D1207260

feast@home

Penguin Books

JULIE LE CLERC

feast @home

PHOTOGRAPHY BRUCE NICHOLSON

contents

acknowledgements | 06
introduction | 07
quick conversions | 11

01 weeknight feasts | 12
02 drinks party | 34
03 smart starters | 58
04 friends for dinner | 78
05 just desserts | 96
06 late suppers | 120
07 celebrations | 140

recipe index | 165

I want to extend my warmest thanks to the
following generous and gifted people who
assisted in making this particular book special.

Thank you to food photographer Bruce Nicholson,
for hours spent in compatible collaboration to
produce these outstanding and engaging food
images. Cheers Bruce! Many thanks, as always,
go to my wonderful publisher and friend, Bernice
Beachman, for your sense of humour, enthusiasm,
and constant support of my work. Thank you
so much Philippa Gerrard, my faithful guardian
angel of production and editor at Penguin, for
all your hard work. Plus, an extra-special thank
you for welcoming us into your lovely home
and lending your gorgeous treasures for
photographic purposes. Grateful thanks go to
Athena Sommerfeld, once again, for a work of
beauty in design. Thank you Helen Dixon for
one last hand-modelling job that you didn't realise
you had. Kind thanks to Anna Bougen for lending
the magnificent lengths of Indian fabric used as
backdrops in some images. And to all my family
and friends, as always, I say a big thank you for
your never-ending patience, understanding and
encouragement. Last but not least, thanks to
Cuisine magazine where some of these recipes
first appeared.

Grateful thanks to these stores for kindly
lending some of the fabrics and tableware used
as photographic props: Madder and Rouge for
enchanting items of beauty. Kate Fitzpatrick
Home for fabric backdrops. Rachel Carley for
exquisite artisan ceramics. St Clare Copperware
for superb and utilitarian copper saucepans.
Sabato Ltd, purveyors of inspiring and delectable
ingredients for the table.

introduction

The pleasures to be gained from relaxed feasting with family and friends are great. In my experience, when lovingly prepared meals are shared in an easygoing way, both the occasion and the dishes become unforgettable. This is why some of the most pleasant recollections I have involve time spent around the table sharing delicious food and good company.

It's also calming to remember that a gathering is not meant to be a culinary competition. Thankfully, the days of painstakingly arranged foods and formal dinner parties are long gone, replaced by the lyrical notion of simply inviting friends around to enjoy a convivial meal.

This book therefore is not about formal entertaining – it is about creating delicious feasts at home for the people you care about. These are smart, practical, stylish recipes covering ideas for every occasion, from simple dinner parties to celebrations, plus comforting evening meals to share with family and friends. This is the type of food that brings people together!

While my previous cookbook and companion volume to this one, *café@home*, concentrated on food for the daylight hours – food we've come to associate with café-style – these pages are dedicated to food to serve in the evening, summer or winter.

When I entertain at home, I favour informal dining experiences. A starter can be as easy as assembling any number of quality Italian ingredients to serve as antipasto, along with some of my home-made dips, such as salsa verde or spiced carrot dip. Sometimes I'll enjoy the creative process of plating courses; other times I'll take the interactive approach and let everyone serve themselves from large platters. Either way, I keep it simple, concentrating on freshness, flavour, and food that engages all the senses.

Cold winter nights are the perfect time to invite friends over to enjoy warm food and company. Light the fire, if you have one, or flood the house with candles, which create a remarkable amount of heat and atmosphere. Serve pre-dinner mulled wine by the fireside – warm, good red wine with an infusion of a cinnamon stick, a few cloves, orange slices and a little sugar to taste, sip and enjoy. Nursery food revisited is a cosy way to end such an evening – self-saucing chocolate hazelnut pudding or macadamia steamed puddings with caramel sauce are guaranteed to please any crowd.

For summer gatherings I aim to combine elegance and freshness. Light, bright foods are what we all want to eat in the summertime. Presentation is effortless because summer food lends itself to casual arrangement on platters. Luxurious piles of sparkling seafood served with simply delicious sauces are easy to compose. Big bowls of salad for all to share make perfect summer meals. Try, for instance, angel hair pasta with smoked tuna and lemon, or a platter of North African eggplant salad with grilled chicken. Dine outdoors and drape flowing lengths of fabric over the dining table to set the scene for pure enjoyment.

Mid-week, or when cooking for family, I find that a combination of innovation mixed with

tradition works well. My smoked fish pie with parsley mash is a good example. This is a timeless dish that I've rearranged and jazzed up with the addition of capers, a lighter sauce and a topping of herb-infused mashed potatoes. For flavoursome, simple yet nurturing weeknight feasts, you can't go past dishes such as Greek meatballs, pumpkin and salami frittata or chicken jambalaya.

Celebrations offer the ultimate chance to show off and cook more over-the-top dishes, such as whole glazed ham or duck with cranberry sauce. I also find that baking a special cake or dessert will invariably be greeted with squeals of delight from young and old alike. Who could resist zuccotto with its velvety centre? My amazing Christmas fruit cake, crisp pavlova with passionfruit curd, and pecan, prune and chocolate celebration cake are all irresistible.

Cooking is an eclectic art and we all gather favourite recipes from friends, family, working kitchens, eating-out experiences and work-mates. I acknowledge the brilliant, bold and generous home cooks and chefs who have influenced my taste-buds over the years. My own constant exploration of ingredients through my extensive travels, reading and experimenting has broadened my personal recipe book.

The fragrance, colour, texture, and especially the flavour of ingredients captivate me. Achieving dishes with seriously good flavour therefore is always my focus when I'm creating or developing recipes. I believe that when good ingredients are cooked in a way that emphasises their natural flavour, texture, aroma and appearance, this will produce a truly memorable meal.

Many years of commercial and private boutique catering have taught me a few tricks as well, and I happily share these here with you. Throughout *feast@home* you will find that I have enhanced each recipe with tips and hints, substitutions and presentation ideas for boosting visual impact. Above all, I believe that the key to easy entertaining is all in the planning. It may seem obvious, but the obvious is often forgotten in the heat of the moment. A little organised forethought – a well-considered menu, and a time-plan – will leave you with more time to mingle with friends and enjoy your own event.

One of the nicest compliments I've ever received was from a customer in a café that I owned at the time. She said, 'When I eat your food I can feel love.' I tend to cook from the heart, and the best advice I can give you is to let your entertaining reflect your own character. You can't go wrong if you entertain according to your own style. Follow recipes that inspire you, and choose to share these with people whose company you enjoy.

Take pleasure, as I do, in welcoming friends and family to your home and table. And remember that any occasion is made extraordinary when beautifully prepared food is served with love. It is my hope that this collection of some of my most favourite recipes will inspire you to cook, entertain and feast @ home.

Julie Le Clerc

quick conversions

weights

30g	1oz
125g	4oz
225g	8oz
450g	1 pound

measures

1 level teaspoon (universal)	5ml
1 level tablespoon (NZ, UK, US)	15ml
1 level tablespoon (Australia)	20ml
1 cup liquid	250ml
4 cups liquid	1 litre
1 pint	600ml

useful equivalents

1 egg white	30g
1 level cup flour	150g
1 level cup sugar	200g

oven temperature guide

Description	°C	°F	Gas Mark
Slow	110–130	225–250	½–1
Moderately slow	140–160	275–325	2–3
Moderate	180–190	350–375	4–5
Moderately hot	190–200	375–400	5–6
Hot	210–240	425–450	7–8
Very hot	250–260	475–500	9–10

As oven models and thermostats vary, these conversions are a guide only. Fan-forced ovens (convection ovens) are usually set lower than conventional ovens. Increase the fan-forced temperature given by 10–20° for conventional ovens or refer to the manufacturer's instructions.

01.wee

knight feasts

Create simple yet nurturing family meals. Time spent at the table is valuable time. Invite friends for a casual mid-week feast peppered with convivial conversation.

+ serving suggestion ... make a sweet potato gratin by cutting peeled sweet potatoes into large chunks. Drizzle with olive oil and roast in a hot oven for 20 minutes. Combine with lots of crushed garlic, season well and place in a gratin dish. Add liquid cream to half-fill dish and bake for 20 minutes until golden brown.

lamb shanks with field mushrooms

Slow-cooked lamb shanks become so meltingly tender that the meat just falls off the bone. And the bones are finger-licking good!

¼ cup flour

sea salt and freshly ground black pepper

4 hind lamb shanks (the hind shanks are bigger)

3–4 tablespoons olive oil

1 large onion, peeled and diced

1 cup red wine

2 cups reduced beef stock

8 field mushrooms

1 Preheat oven to 170°C. Season flour with salt and pepper. Roll lamb shanks in seasoned flour to lightly coat. Heat oil in a frying pan and brown lamb shanks for 1–2 minutes on all sides. Transfer shanks to a casserole dish.

2 Add diced onion to the frying pan and cook over a medium heat for 5 minutes. Add red wine to deglaze the pan, then simmer for 5 minutes. Add stock and bring to the boil, then pour this over the lamb shanks. Cover and bake for 2 hours, turning once during cooking.

3 Brown mushrooms in the frying pan for 1 minute on each side, then add to the casserole dish and cook, uncovered, for a further 30 minutes. Skim sauce of fat and adjust seasoning with salt and pepper to taste.

4 Serve with mashed potatoes or a sweet potato gratin (left). Serve with a palate-cleansing green salad as a separate course if desired.

Serves 4

red lamb curry

Making your own spice paste is a very satisfying process that results in a textural, pungent and vibrantly aromatic base to any home-made curry.

1 large onion, peeled and diced

4cm piece fresh ginger, peeled and roughly chopped

2 cloves garlic, peeled

1–2 small red chillies, seeds removed

¼ cup tomato paste

1 teaspoon each ground cumin, paprika and garam masala

3–4 tablespoons vegetable oil (such as sunflower or olive oil)

800g lamb leg or shoulder steaks, cut into 4cm cubes

1½ cups beef stock

sea salt and freshly ground black pepper

½ cup toasted cashew nuts

¼ cup chopped fresh coriander

steamed basmati rice, to serve

1 Place onion, ginger, garlic, chillies, tomato paste and spices into a food processor and blend to form a paste, or pound with a mortar and pestle.

2 Heat oil in a large saucepan and brown lamb cubes on all sides in 2–3 batches. Remove meat to one side. Add paste mixture to the pan and cook for 1–2 minutes, then add the stock.

3 Return meat to the pan. Bring to the boil, then simmer uncovered for 25 minutes until sauce has thickened and lamb is tender. Season with salt and pepper to taste.

4 Scatter with cashew nuts and coriander and serve with steamed basmati rice.

Serves 4

+ my advice ... home-made curry pastes can last for up to 4 days in the fridge if covered. Leftover paste can be frozen in zip-lock plastic bags for up to 3 months. Flatten the bags well to remove all the air and label with the date of packaging for easy reference.

17

+ how to make ... red pepper purée. Preheat oven to 200°C. Halve 2 red peppers and remove seeds. Place peppers in an oven pan, rub with a little olive oil and bake for 30 minutes or until skins blister. Transfer to a bowl, cover and stand for 10 minutes to sweat, then peel off skins. Place the pepper flesh and 2 cloves of garlic in the bowl of a food processor and purée to form a smooth paste, adding a little extra olive oil if necessary. Season with salt and pepper to taste.

crushed pea pasta with chargrilled lamb cutlets

Peas are a vegetable that most children will eat. Combine peas with the silky texture of orzo and this idea is bound to be a winner.

1^1/$_2$ cups orzo (rice-shaped pasta)

^{1}/$_4$ cup extra virgin olive oil

2 cloves garlic, crushed

1^1/$_2$ cups peas (fresh or frozen)

2 sprigs fresh mint leaves

sea salt and freshly ground black pepper

16 lamb cutlets, French-trimmed

1 Cook orzo in plenty of boiling salted water for 10 minutes or until just tender to the bite. Drain well, toss with olive oil and garlic and cover to keep warm.

2 At the same time, cook peas with mint in boiling salted water for 3–5 minutes or until tender. Drain well, remove mint and crush peas with a fork or potato masher. Combine peas with hot drained pasta and season with salt and pepper to taste.

3 Heat a chargrill pan, barbecue or frying pan. Season lamb cutlets with salt and pepper and brown for 2–3 minutes on each side to cook to medium-rare. Serve on top of crushed pea pasta with red pepper purée on the side.

Serves 4

greek meatballs with tomato and olive sauce

I first ate this traditional Greek dish in the home of my dear friend Donna, who lives in Sydney. Her mother lovingly taught the recipe to Donna, who in turn introduced it to me. This is my version, cooked from my taste memory with grateful thanks to Greek family traditions.

3 slices white bread, crusts removed

1/4 cup sweet wine, marsala or sherry

700g lamb mince

3 cloves garlic, crushed

1 teaspoon ground cinnamon

1 egg, lightly beaten

sea salt and freshly ground black pepper

1/4 cup plain flour

olive oil for frying

1 Soak the bread in the wine for 10 minutes to soften. Break up the bread and combine in a bowl with the lamb mince, garlic, cinnamon and beaten egg, mixing well until blended. Season with salt and pepper.

2 With damp hands, mould walnut-sized portions into balls and set aside on a tray. Roll the balls in the flour to lightly coat.

3 Preheat oven to 180°C. Heat oil in a large frying pan and fry meatballs until golden brown all over (this will need to be done in 2–3 batches). Place meatballs in an oven dish. Pour over tomato and olive sauce.

4 Bake meatballs for 35–40 minutes, stirring once to prevent sticking. Serve with plain rice or pasta, such as orzo.

tomato and olive sauce

400g can chopped tomatoes

1 tablespoon tomato paste

1 tablespoon sugar

1/2 cup hot water

2 tablespoons chopped fresh oregano

3/4 cup green olives, rinsed and drained

sea salt and freshly ground black pepper

1 To make the sauce, combine all ingredients in a bowl, season with salt and pepper to taste and pour over browned meatballs.

Serves 6

+ good idea ... Greek meatballs work well as a cocktail food item; serve them warm, bite-sized and skewered with party picks for eating ease.

+ canned tomatoes ... are an important staple that all self-respecting store cupboards should never be without.

+ Israeli couscous ... has larger grains than Moroccan couscous (above), which is the more common type to be found. Either couscous, however, is perfectly fine to use in this particular dish.

seafood stew with couscous

The addition of couscous transforms this simple seafood stew into a hearty meal.

4 tablespoons olive oil

2 large onions, peeled and diced

4 cloves garlic, peeled and sliced

2 celery sticks or 1 fennel bulb, finely sliced

1 cup dry white wine

$1/4$ teaspoon saffron threads soaked in $1/4$ cup boiling water

800g canned diced tomatoes

2 cups chicken or vegetable stock

juice of 1 lemon

400g mussels, cleaned and beards removed

$1/2$ cup couscous (I used Israeli couscous)

400g prawns, cleaned

400g white-fleshed fish, cut into large cubes

sea salt and freshly ground black pepper

2 tablespoons chopped fresh parsley

1 Heat a very large saucepan, add oil and cook onions, garlic and celery or fennel over a medium heat for 5–10 minutes until softened but not coloured.

2 Add wine, saffron, tomatoes and stock and bring to the boil. Simmer uncovered for 5 minutes to concentrate flavours. Mix in lemon juice.

3 Add the mussels, cover the pan and simmer for 5–10 minutes until shells have opened; discard any that do not open.

4 Add the couscous, prawns and cubed fish. Simmer a further 5–10 minutes with the lid off to cook couscous and fish. Season with salt and pepper to taste and serve scattered with parsley.

Serves 4

fish baked with oregano and tomato juice

This easy, all-in-one fish dish is full of concentrated flavours and yet is virtually fat-free.

1kg (4 large) waxy potatoes, scrubbed

4 large tomatoes, thickly sliced

sea salt and freshly ground black pepper

3 tablespoons chopped fresh oregano

650g boneless, thick, white-fleshed fish fillets, such as
    snapper or cod

juice of 1 lemon

2 cups tomato juice

1 Cook potatoes whole in boiling, salted water until tender. Remove and cut into thick slices. Preheat oven to 200°C.
2 Layer potato and tomato slices in a deep-sided baking dish (e.g. a lasagne dish), seasoning with salt and pepper and oregano between layers. Place fish fillets on top and squeeze lemon juice over fish. Pour in tomato juice to completely cover layered ingredients.
3 Bake for 25 minutes. Serve immediately.

Serves 4

+ my advice ... any type of fish will work well in this dish but it is important to use a waxy variety of potato so that they hold together during cooking. Ask your greengrocer if you're unsure which type of potato would be appropriate.

smoked fish pie with parsley mash

My version of this old-fashioned, favourite, pastry-less pie combines a couple of twists and never fails to delight and satisfy hungry appetites.

800g mashing potatoes, peeled and cooked until tender

50g butter

1/2 cup warmed milk

3 tablespoons chopped fresh parsley

sea salt and freshly ground black pepper

75g butter

1 large onion, chopped

1/4 cup plain flour

2 1/2 cups milk

600g smoked fish, bones removed and flaked

1/3 cup capers, rinsed and drained

2 hard-boiled eggs, quartered (optional)

1 Heat oven to 190°C. Drain potatoes well, then add first measure of butter, milk and parsley, whipping potatoes until smooth and fluffy. Season with salt and pepper to taste.
2 Melt 75g butter in a large saucepan, add onion and cook over a medium heat until softened but not coloured. Stir in flour and cook for one minute. Remove from heat, gradually add milk and whisk to combine. Cook over a medium heat, stirring constantly until the sauce thickens.
3 Remove from heat. Add smoked fish and capers, and chopped eggs if desired. Pour into a deep ovenproof dish or 4 individual large ramekins and pipe or spoon potato over the surface.
4 Bake for 20–30 minutes until potato is golden brown.

Serves 4

+ serving suggestion ... serve steamed greens on the side, such as asparagus or beans in summer; broccoli or Brussels sprouts in winter.

+ Italian risotto rice … is a special type of rice that has the ability to retain its shape and bite while letting out a lot of starch. The starch gives that delightful creamy texture to the finished risotto. For producing excellent risotto, look for Carnaroli, Vialone nano or Arborio rice in supermarkets or specialty food stores.

broccoli and parmesan risotto

Risotto is a wonderfully satisfying dish that lends itself to all kinds of flavourings – here I love the surprisingly peppery green addition of puréed broccoli.

1 head broccoli, roughly chopped
2 cloves garlic, peeled
3 tablespoons olive oil
4½ cups quality chicken stock
3 tablespoons extra virgin olive oil
1 large onion, finely diced
3 cloves garlic, crushed
2 cups Italian risotto rice, such as Carnaroli,
  Vialone nano or Arborio
½ cup dry white wine
½ cup salted capers, rinsed
sea salt and freshly ground black pepper
½ cup grated fresh Parmesan (Parmigiano Reggiano)

1 Cook broccoli in boiling salted water until just tender and still very green. Drain and place in ice cold water to cool, then drain well. Purée in a blender or food processor with the garlic and olive oil, adding a little stock if necessary to blend. Place stock in a small pan and bring to the boil.
2 Heat a large heavy-based pan, add oil, then onion and garlic, and sweat over a medium heat until soft. Add risotto rice and allow to toast but not brown, stirring constantly for 2 minutes.
3 Add wine to the pan and cook until almost completely evaporated. Add a ladleful of hot stock. Stir until the mix is nearly dry, then repeat adding stock until it is all absorbed and the risotto is cooked (this takes 15–20 minutes).
4 Stir in prepared broccoli purée, capers, salt and pepper. Remove pan from the heat, cover and allow risotto to steam for 5 minutes.
5 Stir through Parmesan, adding a little extra hot stock if necessary to create a creamy consistency.

Serves 6

pumpkin and salami frittata

Frittata is a fantastic concept that allows for experimentation – try substituting different vegetables, meats and herbs for the ones given to ring the changes.

300g pumpkin, peeled and cut into 2cm cubes

1 leek, finely sliced

1/4 cup olive oil

6 eggs

1/2 cup milk

1/4 cup cream

1/2 cup grated Cheddar cheese

sea salt and freshly ground black pepper

150g sliced salami

1 tablespoon each chopped fresh basil and parsley

1 Boil or steam pumpkin until just tender. Drain and set aside. Meanwhile, in a 24cm non-stick frying pan with an ovenproof handle, sweat leek in 2 tablespoons of the measured olive oil until softened. Preheat oven to 170°C.

2 In a bowl beat eggs with milk and cream, then stir in cheese. Season well with salt and pepper. Mix in pumpkin, leek, salami and herbs.

3 Place remaining oil in the same frying pan and place over a medium heat. Once hot, pour in frittata mixture. Stir over heat, bringing cooked mixture in from sides of pan to evenly distribute ingredients and partially cook egg. Bake for 35 minutes or until set.

4 Remove from the oven and allow to cool a little before inverting onto a plate to turn out. Flip back to presentation side to serve.

Serves 8

+ serving suggestion ... as a side to frittata, I recommend serving a tossed garden-fresh green salad, drizzled with some aged balsamic vinegar and extra virgin olive oil.

chicken jambalaya

I've received many a compliment about this tasty family meal and you will too!

650g chicken breasts, thinly sliced

olive oil

1 large red onion, diced

2 cloves garlic, chopped

1 red pepper, seeds removed, diced

1 green pepper, seeds removed, diced

3 coarse-textured spicy sausages, such as chorizo, sliced

1 1/2 cups long-grain rice

2 teaspoons paprika

1 1/2 cups tomato purée

2 cups cold water

3 tablespoons chopped fresh parsley

sea salt and freshly ground black pepper

1 Heat a large pan, add a little oil and brown chicken to cook. Place chicken to one side.

2 In the same pan cook onion, garlic and diced peppers for 5 minutes, stirring often. Add spicy sausage, rice and paprika and stir-fry for 1–2 minutes. Add tomato purée and water, bring to the boil, then cover and simmer gently for 20 minutes to cook rice. Remove from the heat.

3 Fluff up rice and stir in chicken, parsley and salt and pepper to taste. Cover and stand for 5 minutes for chicken to warm through. Serve immediately.

Serves 6

+ substitute ... smoky bacon for the sausage if desired. Extra vegetables such as sliced carrots, courgettes, beans, peas or cauliflower can also be added to the mix to make the ultimate all-in-one meal.

+ how to make ... oven-dried tomatoes. Preheat oven to 130°C. Cut a dozen small tomatoes in half and place cut-side-down on paper towels to drain for 5 minutes. Turn tomatoes cut-side-up and transfer to a baking tray lined with non-stick baking paper. Bake slowly for 2 hours or until semi-dried. Remove to cool. Oven-dried tomatoes will last for 2–3 days stored in the fridge.

oven-dried tomato and chicken couscous

Couscous creates a light base for this mélange of textures and flavours, which can be rearranged according to the seasons if so desired.

4 skinless chicken breasts

1 bay leaf

1 cup couscous

1 cup chicken stock

1 bunch asparagus, trimmed and halved

2 cobs corn, kernels removed with a sharp knife

12 oven-dried tomatoes (see note)

1/2 cup dried cranberries, cherries or raisins

1/4 cup each chopped fresh parsley and basil

sea salt and freshly ground black pepper

1 Place chicken breasts and bay leaf in a saucepan and cover with cold water. Bring to the boil, then turn down the heat to barely simmer for 10 minutes. Remove chicken breasts and slice thickly against the grain.

2 At the same time, place couscous in a bowl. Place stock in a saucepan and bring to the boil. Pour hot stock over couscous and stir well. Cover bowl with plastic wrap and leave to steam for 5–10 minutes.

3 Cook asparagus and corn kernels in boiling salted water for 1–2 minutes then drain well.

4 Fluff up couscous with a fork and toss with chicken, asparagus, corn, oven-dried tomatoes, dried cranberries and herbs. Season with salt and pepper to taste and serve hot or cold.

Serves 4

thai curried-chicken pies

Green curries are very aromatic as they are imbued with highly perfumed ingredients such as lemongrass, galangal or ginger, spring onions and basil.

vegetable oil, such as sunflower oil

800g skinless chicken thigh meat, cut into 2cm cubes

50g packet Thai green curry paste (available from supermarkets or Asian stores)

400g can coconut milk

2 pre-rolled sheets puff pastry

1 egg, beaten to glaze

1 Heat a large frying pan, add a little oil and brown cubed chicken in 2–3 batches for 1–2 minutes on each side. Remove to one side. Add curry paste to the pan and cook for 1 minute, stirring constantly.

2 Add coconut milk, whisking to form a smooth sauce. Simmer for 5 minutes, then add chicken. Simmer for another 5 minutes, then remove to a bowl to cool. Refrigerate for at least 45 minutes, or until cold.

3 Divide chicken mixture between 4 1¼-cup capacity ramekins. Cut pastry lids to 1cm larger than circumference of ramekins and secure in place with beaten egg. Crimp edges with a fork and make several incisions in the surface of the pies to release steam during cooking. Chill pies for 30 minutes.

4 Preheat oven to 200°C. Brush pastry lids with beaten egg. Bake pies for 20 minutes or until pastry is golden brown and puffed.

Serves 4

+ shortcut ... incorporating a packet of Thai green curry paste may sound like cheating but believe me, these pastes are very authentic, inexpensive and delicious.

north african eggplant salad with grilled chicken

This is a favourite recipe of mine that I've been making for many years now but have never tired of.

800g (3 medium) eggplants

olive oil

1 teaspoon Spanish sweet smoked paprika

1 teaspoon each ground cumin and coriander

4 skinless chicken breasts

lemon coriander dressing

3 cloves garlic, crushed

3 tablespoons extra virgin olive oil

zest and juice of 2 lemons

¼ cup roughly chopped fresh coriander leaves

sea salt and freshly ground black pepper

1 Preheat oven to 180°C. Slice eggplants into 1cm thick half rounds and brush lightly with olive oil. Mix spices together and rub into aubergine slices. Spread slices on an oven tray and roast for 20–25 minutes until golden brown. Remove to cool.

2 To make the dressing, mix garlic, oil, lemon juice, zest and coriander together. Toss through spiced aubergine. Season to taste with salt and pepper.

3 Preheat oven to 180°C. Heat a chargrill pan or frying pan and brown chicken breasts for 3–4 minutes on each side. Transfer chicken to an oven pan and bake for 5–8 minutes to finish cooking through (depending on size of chicken breasts).

4 Serve the salad at room temperature, with chicken breasts on top.

Serves 4

+ my advice ... slice eggplants with a serrated knife. The sometimes-tough skin of eggplant will quickly blunt a knife's edge, but a serrated edge will cut through with ease.

hokkien noodles with tofu and water chestnuts

The plump and slippery texture of hokkien noodles is the perfect contrast to the wonderful crunch of water chestnuts and stir-fried peppers.

600g hokkien noodles

vegetable oil, such as sunflower or grapeseed oil

1 cup canned whole water chestnuts, drained

2 red peppers, seeds removed, roughly sliced

500g firm tofu, cut into 2cm cubes

1/4 cup hoisin sauce

1/4 cup light soy sauce (or more to taste)

1/4 cup torn fresh basil leaves

2 tablespoons toasted black or white sesame seeds

1 Place noodles in a bowl of hot water for 1 minute to soften and separate, then drain well. Heat a wok, add a little oil and cook drained water chestnuts and pepper pieces for 3–4 minutes, tossing over a high heat until lightly charred. Remove to one side.

2 Add a little more oil and cook the tofu in 2 batches for 3–4 minutes, tossing over a high heat until golden brown.

3 Return the vegetables to the wok with the drained noodles, hoisin and soy sauce and stir-fry for 3–4 minutes until hot. Taste and add more soy sauce to season if necessary. Serve scattered with fresh basil and sesame seeds.

Serves 4

+ substitute ... udon noodles would also work well in this light and deliciously healthy dish.

bacon and avocado burgers

Nothing beats the fun of filling your own burger! And this way you know exactly what has gone into it.

olive oil for frying

1 large red onion, finely chopped

450g beef mince

1 small red chilli, seeds removed, finely chopped

3 tablespoons chopped fresh oregano

sea salt and freshly ground black pepper

8 rashers rindless bacon

4 designer burger buns, sliced in half

1 cup rocket leaves

2 large tomatoes, sliced

1 avocado, peeled and diced

1/4 cup home-made tomato sauce or chutney

1/4 cup sour cream

1 Heat a pan, add a little oil and cook onion over a medium heat for 5 minutes to soften but not colour. Remove to cool.

2 Combine cold onion with beef mince, chilli and oregano, and season well with salt and pepper. Pound the mixture with your fist so that it holds together. Divide mixture into four portions. With damp hands, shape portions into large flat patties.

3 Grill or fry patties in a pan with a little oil for 2–3 minutes on each side until brown. Grill or fry bacon until crisp. Brush burger buns with a little olive oil if desired and toast or grill until golden.

4 Layer rocket leaves, chilli-beef patty, crispy bacon, tomato and avocado on bun bases. Top with tomato sauce and a dollop of sour cream and place lids on buns. Serve immediately.

Serves 4

+ flavour options ... for home-made burgers are endless. Layer up burgers with lots of crisp leaves such as rocket, watercress or specialty lettuces. Lighten up by exchanging the meat for fish, chicken, tofu or grilled vegetables, such as field mushrooms or sliced eggplant. Add some exotic cheeses, such as blue vein, feta or Brie, to melt enticingly onto the bun. And finish it all off with a tasty sauce, relish, chutney and/or a good dollop of basil pesto.

02.drink

Small savoury tastes intermingled with cocktails; shaken or stirred. Delectable morsels to complement fabulous drinks. Cin cin, santé, good health, cheers!

s party

feta and fennel seed dip

This is my personal all-time favourite dip due to its sumptuous texture, rich mouth appeal and salty yet creamy flavour tinged with the refreshing tang of anise.

200g soft cow's feta cheese, crumbled

1 cup sour cream

2 tablespoons fennel seeds, toasted

3 tablespoons extra virgin olive oil

1 In the bowl of an electric mixer beat feta and sour cream together to form a smooth paste. Stir in fennel seeds and olive oil.

2 Serve dip with grisini (bread sticks) or spread on crostini.

Makes 2 cups

spiced carrot dip

Dips are guaranteed crowd pleasers, and provide especially good vegetarian options.

700g (4 large) carrots, peeled and roughly chopped

2 cloves garlic, peeled and roughly chopped

1 teaspoon each toasted ground cumin and coriander

1/4–1/2 cup extra virgin olive oil

sea salt and freshly ground black pepper

1 Cook carrots in boiling salted water until very tender. Drain well and while still warm purée with garlic and spices in a food processor.

2 With the motor running, add enough olive oil to form a smooth and creamy paste. Season with salt and pepper to taste. Refrigerate to cool and serve with grisini (bread sticks), crostini or fresh bread to dip.

Makes 2 cups

+ this goes with that ... spiced carrot dip also makes a luscious salad dressing. Try a dollop over salad greens, simple pasta or roast vegetable salads.

+ how to make ... crostini. Thinly slice sourdough stick, brush lightly with olive oil on both sides and bake in a moderate oven for about 10 minutes or until crisp and golden brown.

bread cups filled with salmon and kaffir lime salad

These appetising mouthfuls combine a wonderful array of tastes and textures.

12 slices white sandwich bread, crusts removed

olive oil

300g very fresh, raw salmon fillet, skin removed

3 spring onions, finely chopped

2 kaffir lime leaves, very finely chopped

juice of 1 lime

1 tablespoon sesame oil

sea salt and freshly ground black pepper

1 Preheat oven to 190°C. Roll out bread slices with a rolling pin to flatten. Cut 5cm circles from each slice and brush with a thin coating of oil. Press into oiled mini-muffin tins and bake for 5–10 minutes until golden. Remove to cool. Store in an airtight container for up to 1 week.
2 Cut salmon into a very small dice. Combine with remaining ingredients and chill well. Serve small mounds of salmon mixture in bread cases.

Makes 24

figs with gorgonzola and prosciutto

These fig parcels can also be baked for 5–10 minutes in a hot oven so that the prosciutto becomes crisp – serve warm and make the most of the short time that figs are in season.

12 fresh figs, cut in half

freshly ground black pepper

100g Gorgonzola

12 slices prosciutto, sliced in half lengthways

1 Season halved figs with freshly ground black pepper. Place a teaspoonful of Gorgonzola on each cut-side.
2 Wrap a length of prosciutto around each fig to serve.

Makes 24

+ my advice ... aim for trays of food to be passed around about every 10–15 minutes. Calculate to make 10–12 items per person for a two-hour party.

+ this goes with that ... alternative fillings for these bread cups include teaspoonfuls of dips such as salsa verde (see page 49), spiced carrot dip (see page 37) or feta and fennel seed dip (see page 37). A dollop of your favourite chutney topped with crumbled feta or shaved Parmesan cheese is another simple yet popular option.

olive paste quesadillas

There's something about the sharp crispness of these simple morsels that makes them as perennially popular as potato chips, only healthier.

8 flour tortillas

1/2 cup olive paste (or substitute any pesto)

1 Spread olive paste evenly over four tortillas. Sandwich together with remaining tortillas.
2 Heat a frying pan and cook tortilla sandwiches for 2–3 minutes on each side until golden brown and crisp. Remove to a board and cut into wedges. Serve warm piled on a plate.

Makes 24

+ my advice ... have a good supply of cocktail napkins at the ready for greasy fingers and some empty bowls for guests to discard olive pips, used skewers or toothpicks.

baby pappadams holding curried scallops

Baby pappadams are available from some specialty Asian food stores. If necessary, full-sized pappadams can be snapped into smaller pieces before frying. While a little irregular in shape, these work just as well.

20 mini pappadams

olive oil for frying

20 scallops, cleaned

1 teaspoon mustard seeds

1 teaspoon each ground coriander and turmeric

1/2 teaspoon chilli powder

1 tablespoon finely grated fresh ginger

3 tablespoons chopped fresh coriander leaves

sea salt and freshly ground black pepper

1 Briefly deep-fry mini pappadams in a saucepan filled with plenty of hot vegetable oil (such as sunflower) until puffed and golden. Remove to drain on paper towels.
2 Heat a little olive oil in a non-stick pan and sear scallops for 2 minutes on each side to lightly cook. Set aside.
3 In the same pan cook mustard seeds in a little oil over a medium heat until they begin to pop. Add spices, ginger, scallops and chopped coriander and toss well. Season with salt and pepper to taste.
4 Place one scallop in each pappadam to serve at room temperature.

Makes 20

+ good idea ... if you like to hold drinks parties regularly, then it's a good idea to invest in a stack of lightweight trays and serving platters large enough to hold a good display of small food items.

tuna kebabs with wasabi and lime mayonnaise

Tuna is best served rare so that it remains delectably moist. Even if you think you don't like rare fish, please resist the temptation to cook this tuna further and ruin a quality product.

800g tuna steaks cut 2cm thick

zest and juice of 1 orange

juice of 1 lemon

2 tablespoons olive oil

1 teaspoon each ground cumin and paprika

2 cloves garlic, crushed

sea salt and freshly ground black pepper

1 Place tuna steaks in a bowl. Sprinkle over orange zest, juices, olive oil, cumin, paprika, garlic and salt and pepper and marinate for 1 hour.
2 Heat a frying pan, add a little oil and sear tuna steaks for 1 minute on each side. Remove to a board and cut into 2cm cubes and skewer each cube.
3 Serve with wasabi and lime mayonnaise on the side to dip.

Makes 30

wasabi and lime mayonnaise

3 egg yolks

1/2 teaspoon salt

1 tablespoon wasabi paste

juice of 1 lime

3/4 cup vegetable oil, such as sunflower oil

1 Place yolks, salt, wasabi and lime juice in the bowl of a food processor and process until pale and foamy, or blend in a bowl with a whisk or hand-held electric beater.
2 With the motor running or while constantly whisking, add oil in a thin and steady stream until combined.
3 Taste and adjust seasoning or add a little extra lime juice if necessary.

Makes 1 1/4 cups

+ my advice ... plan well so that you can enjoy the party too!

+ good idea ... serve nibbles with drinks rather than a starter to make an evening more informal.

asparagus spears with purple olive cream

Purple olive cream is a very versatile sauce. Try serving a spoonful with vegetables or salads, or smother over simply grilled fish, roast chicken or even barbecued steak.

24 spears asparagus, trimmed

1 Blanch asparagus in boiling salted water for 1–2 minutes or until just tender. Drain and immediately plunge into iced water until thoroughly cold. Drain and dry on paper towels.

purple olive cream

1/2 cup pitted Kalamata olives
1/2 cup sour cream
2–3 tablespoons extra virgin olive oil
sea salt and freshly ground black pepper

1 Place olives in the bowl of a food processor and pulse to chop. Add sour cream and olive oil and process to purée into a smooth purple-coloured paste. Adjust seasoning to taste with salt and pepper. Serve as a dip for asparagus.

Makes 1 cup for 24 asparagus spears

+ good idea ... drinks parties are a fun way to entertain and can be less expensive than other functions, such as buffet dinners.

rare beef on rye with horseradish cream

This is a classic and tempting combination of ingredients that always works well with party drinks.

750g eye fillet of beef, at room temperature, trimmed
1/4 cup wholegrain mustard
sea salt and freshly ground black pepper
12 slices rye bread, crusts removed
1/3 cup horseradish cream
fresh dill to garnish

1 Preheat oven to 220°C. Rub meat with wholegrain mustard and season with salt and pepper. Heat a frying pan and sear beef to brown on all sides. Transfer to an oven pan and roast for 20–25 minutes for medium-rare, depending on the thickness of the meat. Remove to rest and allow to cool, then slice thinly.
2 Cut rye bread into small triangles. Arrange a slice of beef on each triangle. Top with a little horseradish cream and garnish with a sprig of dill.

Makes 24

+ my advice ... provide a good amount of food in proportion to alcohol; 4–5 substantial pieces per hour per person is about right.

spicy fish balls on baby lettuce leaves

Baby lettuce leaves make neat and tidy edible vessels for distributing finger food items, such as these fish balls.

1kg boneless white-fleshed fish, such as snapper
  or cod, roughly cubed
1/2 cup fresh breadcrumbs
3 cloves garlic, crushed
1 small red chilli, seeds removed, finely chopped
3cm piece ginger, finely grated
4 spring onions, finely chopped
1/2 cup chopped fresh coriander
juice of 1 lemon
sea salt and freshly ground black pepper
vegetable oil for frying
24 small lettuce leaves, such as heart of cos

1 Place cubed fish in the bowl of a food processor and process to form a rough-textured paste. Transfer to a bowl and combine with breadcrumbs, garlic, chilli, ginger, spring onions, coriander and lemon juice. Season with salt and pepper and mix well. With damp hands shape into walnut-sized balls.
2 Heat a frying pan, add a little oil and gently fry fish balls until browned all over and cooked through. Drain on paper towels.
3 Place warm fish balls in lettuce leaves to serve.

Makes 24

+ my advice ... is to pace the serving of the food, and intersperse hot and cold items.

+ my advice ... serve finger food of a size that is easy for guests to eat while balancing a drink, a napkin, and possibly a handbag in the other hand!

steamed lamb, carrot and ginger dumplings

These wonton-wrapped dumplings can be fried if preferred, but I find the steamed version lighter and more in line with modern healthy eating.

250g lamb mince

2 medium carrots, peeled and finely grated

3 tablespoons finely grated fresh ginger

3 cloves garlic, crushed

1 tablespoon soy sauce

2 teaspoons quality curry powder

1 tablespoon sweet chilli sauce

sea salt and freshly ground black pepper

1 egg

40 wonton wrappers

sweet chilli sauce to dip

1 Place all the ingredients except the wonton wrappers in a bowl and mix together thoroughly.

2 Lay several wonton wrappers on a work surface. Place 1 teaspoon of the filling in the centre of each wrapper. Moisten edges of wrapper with a little water, gather them up and twist to form a bundle. Repeat until all dumplings are complete. Store on a tray lined and covered with plastic wrap until ready to steam.

3 Line a steamer with banana leaves or cabbage leaves to protect the delicate dumplings and arrange wonton dumplings in a single layer, well spaced on the leaves.

4 Place steamer basket over boiling water and steam dumplings for 15 minutes until puffed and opaque. Serve immediately with sweet chilli sauce to dip.

Makes 40

baby potatoes with sour cream and salmon caviar

These delights offer a contrast of texture and taste to a drinks party menu, which should reflect a balance of different foods and flavours.

15 baby potatoes, scrubbed

sea salt

1/3 cup sour cream

1/3 cup salmon caviar

fresh dill to garnish

1 Cook potatoes in boiling salted water until tender. Drain and remove to cool.

2 Cut potatoes in half and place cut-side-down on a tray lined with plastic wrap. Cut or scoop out a small indentation in the top of each potato half.

3 Place about half a teaspoon of sour cream in each indentation and top with half a teaspoon of salmon caviar. Garnish each with a small sprig of dill.

Makes 30

+ my advice ... don't serve too many items that require last-minute assembling as this can be very time consuming. Instead, plan a menu around a few well-chosen, high-impact ideas that can be prepared in advance.

pork and raisin rolls with salsa verde

Whole pork and raisin rolls make a good main-course option. Serve them drizzled with the juices from the pan and creamy mashed potatoes, and steamed greens on the side.

1/2 cup raisins

1/4 cup marsala or sherry

300g pork mince

2 tablespoons chopped fresh sage

sea salt and freshly ground black pepper

4 pork schnitzels

small bunch spinach, stems removed, blanched and
  dried flat on paper towels

olive oil for frying

1 Place raisins in a bowl with marsala and leave to soak for at least 1 hour.
2 Place pork mince with sage in a bowl and mix well to combine. Season with salt and pepper.
3 Pound schnitzels to flatten and form into rectangles. Spread half the mince mixture over most of each schnitzel, leaving a 2cm border down one long side. Place spinach over mince, then add some raisins. Roll up each parcel into a log and tie with string to secure.
4 Preheat oven to 200°C. Heat an ovenproof frying pan, add a little oil and brown rolls on all sides over a medium heat. Place in the oven for 10 minutes. Remove and cool a little before slicing each roll into 6–7 portions. Serve with salsa verde to dip.

Makes 24-28

salsa verde

3 cloves garlic, peeled

3/4 cup parsley

1/4 cup mint leaves

1/4 cup basil leaves

1/4 cup capers, rinsed and drained

150ml olive oil

sea salt and freshly ground black pepper

1 Place garlic, herbs and capers in the bowl of a food processor and blend until well chopped.
2 With motor running, slowly pour in the oil until well combined and a vibrant green sauce results. Adjust seasoning to taste.

Makes 1 cup

+ my favourite ... manual food processor is a mortar and pestle. Electric food processors are a brilliant invention, but sometimes nothing beats the therapy of pounding fragrant ingredients by hand.

shots of clear gazpacho

This recipe is an adaptation of one by Lorna Wing, an extraordinary cook who used to run a fabulous catering company in London.

1kg vine-ripened tomatoes, quartered

1 tablespoon sea salt

floating vegetable garnish

1 fleshy tomato, skin and seeds removed

1/4 cucumber, seeds removed

1/2 yellow pepper, seeds removed

finely snipped chives

sea salt and freshly ground black pepper

1 Line a sieve with muslin and place over a bowl. Blend tomatoes and salt in a food processor, then pour into prepared sieve. Cover with a plate to gently press and leave overnight for the liquid to drip through.

2 Next day remove pulp (see note below) and reserve the resulting 'tomato water'.

3 Finely dice the garnish vegetables and season with salt and pepper if necessary. Serve tomato water chilled in shot glasses and topped with garnish, which will be suspended in liquid.

Makes 25

+ good idea ... don't discard the tomato pulp which is a by-product of this process, as this can be used for a tomato-based sauce or added to a soup or stew.

goats' cheese and oven-dried tomatoes in basil leaves

Quality goats' cheese is a beautiful thing but if it is not on your list of favourite foods, try substituting cream cheese, feta or any other soft cheese.

120g soft goats' cheese, at room temperature

2 tablespoons lemon juice

20 large unblemished basil leaves

10 red cherry tomatoes, oven-dried for 1 hour
  (see note page 28)

sea salt and freshly ground black pepper

1 In a small bowl mix the goats' cheese with the lemon juice.

2 Lay the basil leaves on a work surface. Place 1 teaspoon of the cheese mixture on each basil leaf, top with an oven-dried cherry tomato and season with salt and pepper.

Makes 20

+ my advice ... if the drinks party is to last for the entire evening then the food needs to be more substantial. I suggest setting up a grazing food station, such as a glazed ham on the bone with fresh crusty bread and chutney.

+ how to make … Parmesan shortbread. Place 1 cup flour, a good pinch each of salt and chilli powder and 100g cubed butter in the bowl of a food processor; process until the mixture resembles fine breadcrumbs. Add $1/2$ cup grated Parmesan and $1/2$ cup grated Cheddar cheese; pulse to combine into pastry. On a lightly floured surface, roll pastry out to 5mm thick. Stamp out discs using a 3cm cutter; place on lightly greased baking sheets, prick gently and chill for 30 minutes. Bake at 190°C for 5–10 minutes until golden.

oysters with gazpacho salsa

The clean, clear flavours of gazpacho perfectly complement those of steely, ice-cold oysters.

2 dozen oysters in the half-shell, chilled
2 tomatoes, peeled, seeds removed, finely diced
¼ telegraph cucumber, seeds removed, finely diced
½ red pepper, seeds removed, finely diced
1 clove garlic, crushed
4 tablespoons extra virgin olive oil
sea salt and freshly ground black pepper
lemon wedges to serve

1 Remove any grit from the oysters and arrange on a serving platter over crushed ice or rock salt to stabilise the shells on the tray.
2 Combine tomatoes, cucumber, red pepper, garlic and olive oil in a bowl and season with salt and pepper.
3 Spoon a little salsa over each oyster. Serve with lemon wedges.

Makes 24

kir

Kir is evocatively French and my most favourite tipple that I can't resist ordering the minute I arrive in Paris.

30ml crème de cassis
200ml sauvignon blanc

1 Pour crème de cassis into a glass. Top up with chilled sauvignon blanc.

Serves 1

+ substitute ... if sauvignon blanc is replaced with champagne or sparkling wine then this is known as Kir Royale.

+ good idea ... for a cosy drinks party, recruit willing volunteers, family or friends to help hand around trays of food while they circulate and chat. Hire help for more formal occasions or when catering for large numbers.

margarita

Once again, classics rule – it's hard to beat the vibrancy of a Margarita!

1/2 cup sugar

pinch salt

juice of 3 lemons

juice of 3 limes

2 slices lemon for glasses

salt for glasses

3/4 cup tequila

3/4 cup crushed ice

1 Place sugar, salt and juices in a saucepan and bring to the boil. Turn down the heat to simmer for 1–2 minutes or until liquid forms a light syrup. Remove to cool and store in the fridge.

2 Sprinkle salt 5mm deep on a plate. Rub rims of Margarita glasses with sliced lemon, then dip in the salt to encrust the rims.

3 Place cold sugar syrup, tequila and crushed ice in a blender. Blend to combine, then pour into salt-rimmed Margarita glasses.

Serves 4

strawberry sangria

Sipping strawberry-scented sangria is a most refreshing and flavoursome way to share time with friends!

750ml bottle dry red wine

1/4 cup Cointreau or brandy

1/4 cup sugar

1 orange, sliced and seeds removed

1 cup strawberries, hulled and halved

2 cups soda water

ice to serve

1 Pour wine into a large jug. Add Cointreau and sugar and stir to dissolve. Add sliced fruit and chill for 1 hour.

2 When ready to serve, add soda water and stir to combine. Pour over ice to serve.

Serves 6

+ my advice ... as a rule of thumb, calculate a minimum of 3 types of glassware per person. For a casual drinks party, you'll need tumblers for water and non-alcoholic drinks, flutes for sparkling wine, and wine glasses.

+ good idea ... for larger gatherings, hire glasses and bar equipment if necessary. Trying to juggle serving drinks and food is a glitch for many people. I recommend delegating this role so that you can concentrate on the food.

03.Sl

Small but perfectly formed appetisers are the best introduction to a meal. These chic first impressions set the scene for the menu to follow.

mart
starters

prawns with coconut and coriander dipping sauce

Place finger bowls laced with lemon wedges on the table by each person so they can cleanse their hands after the sticky business of peeling prawns.

20 raw tiger prawns

1 Heat a hot barbecue, chargrill pan or frying pan and cook prawns for 1–2 minutes on each side. Serve with dipping sauce.

Serves 4

coconut and coriander dipping sauce

2 small green chillies, seeds removed
2 cloves garlic, peeled
1 teaspoon salt
1/2 cup lime juice
1 cup roughly chopped fresh coriander leaves
1 cup desiccated coconut
3/4 cup coconut cream

1 Place chillies, garlic and salt in the bowl of a food processor and pulse to chop. Add lime juice, coriander and coconut and process well to combine.
2 Lastly pulse in coconut cream. Serve as a dip or sauce for prawns.

Makes about 1 1/2 cups

+ this goes with that ...
coconut and coriander dipping sauce also makes an excellent dressing for dishes such as roast chicken or chicken and vegetable salad, seared fresh tuna, steamed asparagus or Asian greens.

+ my favourite ... cook's tools
are my professional knives.
With a good knife in hand,
copious manual food-processing
feats can be achieved. Choose
a small range of knives and
care for them well; in return
they will give you good service
and last a lifetime.

prawn rice paper rolls

Rice paper can be a little tricky to use the first
time round; it is advisable to only work with one
sheet at a time until you master the technique.

18 short bamboo skewers
18 king prawns, peeled and deveined
juice of 1 lime
bunch Vietnamese mint or ordinary mint leaves
18 round sheets rice paper
Thai sweet chilli sauce, soy or hoisin sauce for dipping

1 Skewer prawns lengthways so that they form a straight
line (they will set in this shape once cooked). Heat 3cm
water in a deep-sided frying pan and add the lime juice to
acidulate the water. Add prawns and simmer for 1–2
minutes or until prawns turn bright pink. Remove to a
plate to cool a little, then cover and refrigerate until cold.
Remove skewers once cold.
2 Fill a large bowl with lukewarm water. Place one piece
of rice paper in this water for 1–2 minutes to soften. Lay
sheet of softened rice paper on a clean tea towel. Place
one prawn and a couple of mint leaves in the centre.
Fold in ends and roll up firmly to secure the filling.
Repeat process for remaining rice paper sheets.
3 Serve 3 rolls per person with Thai sweet chilli sauce,
soy sauce or hoisin sauce on the side for dipping.

Serves 6

+ this goes with that ... other filling
suggestions include vermicelli noodles
and vegetables such as finely sliced
carrots, celery, red pepper and bean
sprouts; shredded poached chicken
and vegetables and sweet basil; stir-
fried beef or pork and fresh coriander.

shaved corn, prawn and rocket salad with corn and dill aioli

Salads are favourites for summer entertaining.

20 king prawns, heads and shells removed leaving
 tails intact
2 cobs fresh corn
1 red onion, peeled and very finely sliced
1/2 cup quality sun-dried tomatoes, halved
1 cos lettuce, leaves separated and washed

1 Place 3cm of water in a large saucepan and bring to the boil. Add the prawns and turn off the heat. Remove prawns after 2–3 minutes or when they have turned a deep pink, which means they are just cooked through. Set aside to cool. With a sharp knife, remove the dark veins running down the back of each prawn.
2 Steam or boil corn cobs for 5 minutes, drain and cool. Once cold, remove kernels by shaving from cobs with a sharp knife.
3 Toss cold prawns and corn kernels with remaining salad ingredients in a bowl and serve with corn and dill aioli on the side.

corn and dill aioli

2 egg yolks
juice of 1 lemon
sea salt
3 cloves garlic, peeled
1/2 cup raw corn kernels, cut from the cob
1 tablespoon chopped fresh dill
1/2 cup extra virgin olive oil

1 Place egg yolks and lemon juice in the bowl of a food processor with a little salt and process until pale and fluffy. Add the garlic, corn and dill to the bowl and pulse to combine.
2 With the motor running, slowly drizzle in olive oil until amalgamated and mixture is thick and creamy.

Serves 4

+ substitute ... to reduce the amount of oil in a salad dressing, use herbs, citrus rind and spices to provide flavour instead of fat. Another fat-cutting idea is to replace, for instance, this creamy, mayonnaise-style dressing with low-fat yoghurt, mixed with the same flavourings.

mussels poached in sparkling wine

Cooking with wine can transform the flavour of the humblest to the most lavish of dishes.

2 cups sparkling wine

1 small onion, roughly chopped

1kg fresh mussels, beards removed and scrubbed

1/2 cup cream

1 red pepper, seeds removed, finely diced

1 chilli, seeds removed, chopped

1/4 cup chopped fresh coriander

sea salt and freshly ground black pepper

lemon wedges to serve

1 Place sparkling wine and onion in a large saucepan and bring to the boil. Add mussels, then cover and steam for 2–3 minutes until mussels open. Remove to a serving bowl. Discard any unopened mussels.

2 Strain wine and discard onion. Return wine to a saucepan and bring it to the boil. Cook to reduce by half. Add cream and reduce by half again. Add diced red pepper, chilli, coriander and salt and pepper to taste. Pour sauce over mussels and serve immediately.

Serves 4

+ my advice ... the addition of good wine to cooking, like any quality ingredient, will enhance the taste of a dish. While not completely breaking the bank, don't compromise flavour by adding a poor quality wine to any dish.

scallop and courgette salad

Cold starters make for easy serving and allow the cook time to concentrate on the hot main course.

olive oil

300g fresh scallops

1/2 cup podded broad beans, blanched (frozen are fine)

600g courgettes, trimmed

lime dressing

zest and juice of 2 limes

3–4 tablespoons extra virgin olive oil

sea salt and freshly ground black pepper

1 Heat a non-stick frying pan, add a little oil and brown scallops in batches for 1–2 minutes on each side. Remove to a plate to cool. Peel shells from broad beans to reveal the bright green inner beans.

2 Cut the flesh of the courgettes into long thin strips – this can be done quickly with a special julienne-style peeler or a mandoline, or carefully with a sharp knife. Place courgette strips in a bowl with the scallops and broad beans.

3 Combine lime dressing ingredients, pour over salad and toss well. Check and adjust seasoning if necessary.

Serves 4

scallops in the half-shell with hazelnut pesto

This is my rendition of a tantalising combination I once tasted (well, more than once actually) during a food lover's tour of Adelaide. The heady combination of roasted nuts and perfumed basil sizzling over the sweet, creamy flesh of scallops is completely irresistible.

hazelnut pesto

2 well-packed cups fresh basil leaves

2 cloves garlic, peeled

1/4 cup freshly grated Parmesan

1/2 cup toasted hazelnuts

1/2 cup olive oil

sea salt and freshly ground black pepper

1 Place basil and garlic cloves in the bowl of a food processor and pulse to chop.
2 Add Parmesan and hazelnuts and blend to a pulp.
3 With motor running, slowly drizzle in olive oil, scraping down sides of the bowl. Process to form a smooth paste. Adjust seasoning with salt and pepper to taste.

Makes 1 cup

24 scallops

8 half scallop shells, scrubbed clean

lemon wedges to garnish

1 Preheat a grill on high. Place scallop shells on an oven tray. Arrange 3 scallops in each shell and top with a dollop of hazelnut pesto.
2 Place baking tray under hot grill and cook for 3–4 minutes or until pesto bubbles and turns golden brown. Serve immediately with lemon wedges to garnish.

Serves 4

+ my advice ... cover pesto with a thin film of olive oil to prevent discoloration. This way pesto keeps well in the fridge for 2–3 weeks.

warm prosciutto-wrapped goats' cheese and roast pear salad

Salads are where the seasonal changes in produce are tastefully revealed; this is a quintessentially autumnal combination.

3 pears, halved

olive oil

sea salt and freshly ground black pepper

200g goats' cheese, sliced into 6 equal portions

6 slices prosciutto

1/2 cup toasted hazelnuts

75g baby rocket leaves

1/4 cup hazelnut oil

1 Preheat oven to 220°C. Rub pear halves with olive oil, season with salt and pepper and place in an oven pan. Roast for 15 minutes or until golden brown. Remove to cool to room temperature.
2 Wrap each portion of goats' cheese in a slice of prosciutto. Heat a frying pan, add a little oil and brown these parcels for 1–2 minutes on each side. Remove to drain on paper towels.
3 Assemble salads by arranging one pear half and one goats' cheese parcel on each individual plate. Scatter with hazelnuts and rocket leaves, season with salt and pepper and drizzle with hazelnut oil to serve.

Serves 6

+ visual impact ... plan the way you want the food to look on the plates, and present all portions in the same formation so that the meals are stylishly linked.

+ my advice ... here are some signs to look for to ensure freshness when purchasing whole fish: check that the flesh feels firm when pressed; the eyes are bright and full (not sunken); and the gills are bright red; and fresh fish should smell of nothing but the sea.

teriyaki salmon

Keeping it simple makes fish the ultimate, healthy, and fast meal solution.

600g fresh salmon fillet, skin and pin bones removed
  (see page 149)
1 cup light soy sauce
2 tablespoons finely grated ginger
3/4 cup mirin (sweetened rice wine) or substitute
  sweet sherry
vegetable oil for frying, such as sunflower or grapeseed oil
3 tablespoons black or white sesame seeds, toasted

1 Slice salmon fillet into 4 equal portions and place in a deep-sided ceramic dish. Combine soy, ginger and mirin and pour over salmon. Leave to marinate for one hour.
2 Heat a non-stick frying pan, add a little oil and sear salmon for 1 minute on each side for medium-rare. Scatter with toasted sesame seeds to serve.

Serves 4

+ serving suggestion ... serve teriyaki salmon with a simple salad of baby lettuce leaves dressed with a little lemon juice and sesame oil to complement the salty flavours of the marinade.

lime-marinated fish salad

This compelling fish salad makes an ideal starter to a summer meal but also works as a light lunchtime dish.

600g extremely fresh, white-fleshed fish fillets,
  such as snapper or cod
1/2 cup fresh lime juice
2 cloves garlic, chopped
1 small red onion, finely chopped
3 tomatoes, peeled, seeded and chopped
1/2 cup tomato juice
4 tablespoons chopped fresh coriander
1 teaspoon chopped fresh chilli
2 tablespoons olive oil
1 teaspoon sugar
1/2 teaspoon salt
finely grated zest of 1 lime

1 Cut fish fillets into strips 1cm thick and place in a non-metallic bowl with lime juice. Cover and leave to marinate in the fridge for 2 hours.
2 Mix through remaining ingredients and serve.

Serves 4

+ my advice ... when purchasing fresh fish fillets, look for fillets that are plump and juicy, and smell of fresh seawater.

antipasto salad

This salad arrangement is a quick and simple idea using whatever is available at the deli.

8 slices prosciutto

150g bocconcini (baby mozzarella balls) or
  150g marinated feta

1 cup mixed olives

2 roasted red peppers or 4 Piquillo pimientos

1/2 cup semi-dried tomatoes

sea salt and freshly ground black pepper

1/2 cup basil pesto

1/4 cup extra virgin olive oil

fresh sage or basil leaves to garnish

1 Arrange various antipasto ingredients on individual plates. Season with salt and pepper.
2 Combine basil pesto and olive oil and drizzle over salads. Garnish with fresh sage or basil leaves.

Serves 4

+ substitute ... other store-bought deli ingredients for the ones suggested. Try for instance caper berries, goats' cheese, marinated artichoke hearts or mushrooms, salami, black olive paste, hummus, or other interesting pastes, chutneys or salsas.

eggplant, pepper, courgette and feta terrine

The appealing arrangement of this terrine is as satisfying as its taste.

500g (1 large) eggplant, trimmed

500g (3–4) courgettes, trimmed

olive oil

6 roasted and peeled red peppers (see note below)

200g feta, sliced 5mm thick

1/2 cup basil leaves

sea salt and freshly ground black pepper

basil leaves to garnish

1 Thinly slice eggplant and courgettes lengthways. Brush slices with a little olive oil and cook under a hot grill for 3–4 minutes on each side (this may need to be done in 2–3 batches). Remove to cool.
2 Line a terrine or loaf tin with plastic wrap, leaving an overhang. Alternate layers of roast peppers, eggplant, courgette, feta and basil leaves to fill the terrine, seasoning with a little salt and pepper between layers. Cover filling with the overhang of plastic wrap. Place a weight on top (for example canned products) and refrigerate for 24 hours.
3 Remove the weight, invert the terrine onto a platter and discard the plastic wrap. Carefully cut 2cm thick slices to serve garnished with basil leaves.

Serves 8

+ how to ... roast peppers. Remove the core, seeds and white ribs from peppers before roasting them. Place halved red peppers in an oven pan, rub with a little olive oil and roast at 200°C for 30 minutes, or until the skins blister and the flesh is soft. Remove to a bowl, cover with plastic wrap so that the peppers sweat and the skins loosen. Once cool enough to handle, the skins can easily be slipped off.

chicken and spinach salad with japanese-style dressing

Inspired by Japanese flavours, this salad is almost a free-form medley of sushi filling ingredients, minus the rice.

3 skinless chicken breasts

2 tablespoons sesame oil

150g baby English spinach

1 red pepper, seeds removed, finely sliced

1/4 cup Japanese pickled ginger, cut into strips

2 sheets nori seaweed, cut into fine strips, to serve

japanese-style dressing

1/4 cup mirin (sweetened rice wine)

1 tablespoon sesame oil

2 tablespoons Japanese soy sauce

1 tablespoon lemon juice

1 tablespoon each black and white sesame seeds, toasted

1 Slice chicken into strips. Heat a frying pan with sesame oil and stirfry chicken for 5 minutes to cook. Remove to cool. Toss cold chicken strips, spinach, sliced pepper and pickled ginger in a large bowl.

2 Whisk dressing ingredients together, drizzle over salad and toss well. Arrange on a serving platter and sprinkle with nori to serve.

Serves 4

+ my advice … menu planning is very important. Aim for balance and try to serve courses of different textures (not all crunchy or all smooth foods), stimulating colours, richness (don't add cream to every course for example), and temperature (for instance, serve a cold starter, hot main and warm dessert).

coconut chicken salad in a leaf

I love how these leaves contain and present the salad and yet remain an integral part of the edible dish.

3 skinless chicken breasts

2 stalks lemongrass, crushed

1/2 cup desiccated thread coconut

1/2 cup mung bean sprouts

100g snow peas, finely sliced

1 red pepper, seeds removed, finely sliced

3 spring onions, finely sliced

1 small red chilli, finely sliced

1 kaffir lime leaf, very finely sliced

1/4 cup chopped fresh coriander

6–12 small lettuce leaves

coconut dressing

1/2 cup coconut milk

juice of 1 lime

2 tablespoons grated fresh ginger

1–2 tablespoons Thai fish sauce to taste

1 Place chicken breasts in a saucepan with crushed lemongrass and cover with cold water. Bring to the boil then turn down the heat to gently simmer for 10 minutes. Discard lemongrass, remove chicken to a bowl and cover with cooking liquid to cool. Once cold, refrigerate in liquid.

2 Slice chicken in fine strips and combine with remaining salad ingredients, except lettuce leaves.

3 Combine dressing ingredients, adding fish sauce to taste. Pour dressing over salad and toss well. Arrange 1–2 salad leaves on individual plates. Divide chicken salad by 6, placing a mound on each leaf to serve.

Serves 6

+ my advice … allow plenty of time to glamorise the table (and yourself) before you greet your guests.

salad caprise

The quality of the ingredients makes or breaks this salad. The seductive taste and texture of imported, real buffalo mozzarella combined with sun-ripe tomatoes and basil is beyond sublime.

4 medium vine-ripened tomatoes, sliced

300g buffalo mozzarella, quartered

1 cup fresh basil leaves

sea salt and freshly ground black pepper

extra virgin olive oil

quality aged balsamic vinegar

1 Arrange tomatoes, mozzarella and basil leaves in rows on 4 individual plates. Season with salt and pepper.
2 Serve shot glasses of balsamic vinegar and extra virgin olive oil on the side to drizzle over salad if desired.

Serves 4

+ **visual impact** ... there are two ways to present a compilation such as this: one is to casually toss and naturally place on the plate, but I've opted for a simple arrangement of each ingredient, which just happens to resemble the Italian flag!

courgette and parmesan soup

Serve small amounts of soup as a starter, as it tends to be filling – I find elegant coffee cups and saucers are just the right size.

2 tablespoons olive oil

2 tablespoons butter

2 onions, peeled and chopped

4 cloves garlic, chopped

600g (2 large) mashing potatoes, peeled and roughly chopped

4 cups chicken or vegetable stock (plus extra if
  necessary to thin)

800g (8 medium) courgettes, trimmed and roughly chopped

1 tablespoon fresh thyme leaves

1/4 cup cream cheese

1/4 cup grated fresh Parmesan

sea salt and freshly ground black pepper

extra shaved Parmesan to serve

1 Heat a large saucepan, add oil, butter, onions and garlic, and cook over a medium heat for 10 minutes, stirring regularly until softened but not coloured.
2 Add potatoes and stock, bring to the boil, then simmer for about 10 minutes or until potatoes are soft. Add courgettes and thyme and simmer for 3–4 minutes until courgettes are just tender but still a vibrant green.
3 Purée soup in a blender, adding cream cheese, Parmesan and extra stock to thin if necessary. Season to taste with salt and pepper. Gently reheat to serve topped with extra shaved Parmesan if desired.

Serves 4

+ **my advice** ... simmer rather than boil soups to gently extract the most flavour from the ingredients.

courgette and parmesan soup

+ my advice ... wrap rinds of Parmesan in plastic wrap and store in the freezer for future use in cooking. The addition of Parmesan rind lends a piquant, cheesy flavour to many slow-cooked dishes such as hearty stocks, soups and stews.

04. frie dinner

nds for

Welcome friends to your home and to your table. Relax into fuss-free entertaining. Focus on vivid flavours and presentation. Enjoy good company.

snapper with sweet and sour onions

Full of enticing sweet-sour flavours and vibrant colour, this fish dish always wins great praise.

olive oil for frying

3 medium onions, finely sliced

1/2 teaspoon saffron threads dissolved in 1/4 cup boiling water

1 cup dry white wine

2 tablespoons white wine vinegar

2 tablespoons sugar

1/4 cup dried currants

1/4 cup capers, drained

sea salt and freshly ground black pepper

flour for dusting fish

800g skinless snapper fillets, cut into 8 portions

1 Cook onions in a pan with 2–3 tablespoons oil for 10 minutes to soften but not brown. Add saffron, wine, vinegar and sugar, and bring to the boil. Simmer until syrupy, then add currants and capers, and season to taste.

2 Season flour with salt and pepper and use this to dust fish fillets. Heat a large frying pan with a little oil. Panfry fish over medium heat for 3–4 minutes on each side, depending on thickness of fish, until cooked through.

3 Place fish immediately on a serving dish and pile with sweet and sour onions. Mashed potatoes complement this dish well.

Serves 4

+ how to make ... great mashed potatoes. Cut 1kg peeled, floury-textured potatoes into large chunks. Cook in boiling salted water until tender. Drain potatoes and return to the pan over a low heat, shaking to dry. Remove from the heat and mash or mouli to remove lumps. Add 75g butter and enough warmed milk to whip to a fluffy, creamy consistency. Season well.

saffron tuna with pinot noir lentils

The key to cooking fish well is all in the timing: fish must be cooked quickly and carefully for optimum results. Overcooking destroys the delicacy and moisture of any fish.

4 tablespoons olive oil

2 tablespoons lemon juice

1/4 teaspoon saffron threads

600g fresh tuna, cut into 4 portions

1 1/2 cups Puy lentils

1 bay leaf

1 1/2 cups pinot noir

4 tomatoes, seeds removed, chopped

4 tablespoons chopped fresh dill

sea salt and freshly ground black pepper

olive oil for frying

50g rocket leaves to serve

1 In a small pan briefly heat olive oil, lemon juice and saffron to infuse flavours. Pour over tuna, cover and refrigerate to marinate for 2 hours or overnight.

2 Place lentils and bay leaf in a saucepan and cover generously with cold water. Bring to the boil, then simmer for 20 minutes or until just tender. Drain well.

3 Heat wine in a saucepan and simmer to reduce to 1/2 cup. Add lentils, chopped tomatoes and dill and heat through. Season with salt and pepper to taste.

4 When ready to serve, heat a frying pan with a little olive oil. Remove tuna from marinade, season with salt and pepper and brown for 1–2 minutes on each side (depending on thickness) for medium-rare. Serve tuna on top of lentils and decorate with rocket.

Serves 4

mustard-crusted salmon with asparagus and lemon sauce

This sauce is an invention of mine that is almost like a back-to-front method of making hollandaise sauce. I've also upped the citrus content to give it more zing.

800g salmon fillet, pin bones removed (see page 149)

2 tablespoons wholegrain mustard

sea salt and freshly ground black pepper

olive oil

400g fresh asparagus, trimmed

1 Preheat oven to 200°C. Cut salmon into 4 portions, spread with mustard, season with salt and pepper and place in a lightly oiled roasting pan. Roast for 10 minutes until cooked to medium.

2 Blanch asparagus in boiling salted water for 2 minutes, then drain well. Arrange on serving plates.

3 To serve, place salmon on asparagus and drizzle with lemon sauce.

lemon sauce

200g butter

juice of 2 lemons

$1/2$ teaspoon salt

1 egg yolk

1 tablespoon cream

1 Melt butter with the lemon juice and salt in a pan over a low heat. Mix egg yolk with cream in a bowl, then pour melted butter and lemon onto yolks and whisk together.

2 Return to the pan and heat very gently, whisking until sauce thickens. Do not boil.

Serves 4

+ my advice ... above all, the fish you're cooking needs to be fresh. If you can't catch your own, buy fish from a reliable fishmonger who you know has a high turnover of product.

szechuan-spiced twice-roasted duck

Duck is my all-time favourite main course ingredient. I'll almost always choose it off a menu, and I always enjoy cooking and serving duck to my own dinner guests.

2 onions, quartered

4 star anise

$1/4$ cup hoisin sauce

$1/4$ cup light soy sauce

4 duck legs

$1/2$ teaspoon Szechuan peppercorns, toasted and ground

2 teaspoons Chinese five-spice powder

1 tablespoon sea salt flakes

1 tablespoon each black and white sesame seeds

1 Preheat oven to 200°C. Place onions and star anise in a deep-sided oven pan and drizzle with hoisin and soy sauces. Place duck legs skin-side-down around the vegetable base and fill the pan with water to half cover duck legs. Roast for 45 minutes.

2 Transfer duck legs skin-side-up to a low-sided oven pan. Reserve the stock for another dish. Combine Szechuan pepper, five-spice powder and salt and rub over duck legs. Return to the oven for 30 minutes for skin to crisp. Scatter with sesame seeds 5 minutes before end of cooking so that these toast.

3 Serve with egg noodles simply dressed with sesame oil and steamed broccoli or Asian greens or rice.

Serves 4

+ good idea ... the duck stock formed from braising the duck can be strained and skimmed and used for another dish, for instance, add noodles to create a simple duck noodle soup. Season with extra soy sauce to taste.

slow-cooked ginger chicken

This is an unusual recipe in that the sauce is reduced to almost nothing (this adds a nutty flavour to the dish) and then reconstituted. Sounds weird, but it works!

5cm piece fresh ginger, peeled and roughly chopped

2 cloves garlic, peeled

3 spring onions, chopped

1 large red chilli, roughly chopped

400ml can coconut cream

2 teaspoons cumin seeds, toasted

1 teaspoon ground coriander

1/2 teaspoon ground turmeric

4 skinless chicken Marylands (thigh and drumstick)

1 tablespoon vegetable oil, such as sunflower
  or grape seed oil

2 cinnamon sticks

20 fresh curry leaves

1 Place ginger, garlic, spring onions and chilli in a food processor and blend to a paste. Add coconut cream, cumin, coriander and turmeric and blend well.
2 Joint the chicken legs. Heat a large pan, add oil, cinnamon sticks and curry leaves and cook briefly before adding the coconut cream mixture. Bring to the boil, then add the chicken, turning to coat. Simmer gently, uncovered, for 1 hour, stirring regularly so the sauce does not stick and burn.
3 The chicken will be golden and the coconut milk evaporated, leaving an oil residue. Pour off the oil, return to the heat and add 1/2 cup water to reform a sauce. Serve the chicken and sauce with rice and steamed greens.

Serves 4

chicken with chorizo, tomato and bay leaves

Chorizo is a secret flavour weapon that exudes all its piquancy into this chicken dish.

4 chicken breasts

2 chorizo, sliced diagonally

2 small tomatoes, halved and sliced

12 fresh bay leaves

olive oil

sea salt and freshly ground black pepper

1 Preheat oven to 200°C. Cut 3 diagonal slashes in each chicken breast and place in a low-sided oven pan. Insert a slice of chorizo, tomato and a bay leaf in each slash. Drizzle with oil and season with salt and pepper.
2 Bake for 15–20 minutes, depending on size of chicken breasts. Remove chicken to rest and keep warm for 5 minutes before serving. Serve with steamed greens such as asparagus, beans or Brussels sprouts.

Serves 4

+ serving suggestion ... serve with fragrant lemon rice. Rinse 1 cup basmati rice until the water runs clear. Place rice and the juice and finely grated rind of 2 lemons in a saucepan and cover with cold water so that it rises 3cm above the level of the rice. Cover and cook over a medium heat for 10–15 minutes until all the water has been absorbed. Remove from the heat and leave to steam for 5 minutes. Fluff up the rice with a fork just before serving.

+ visual impact ... make any meal special by using your best tableware and dining by candlelight.

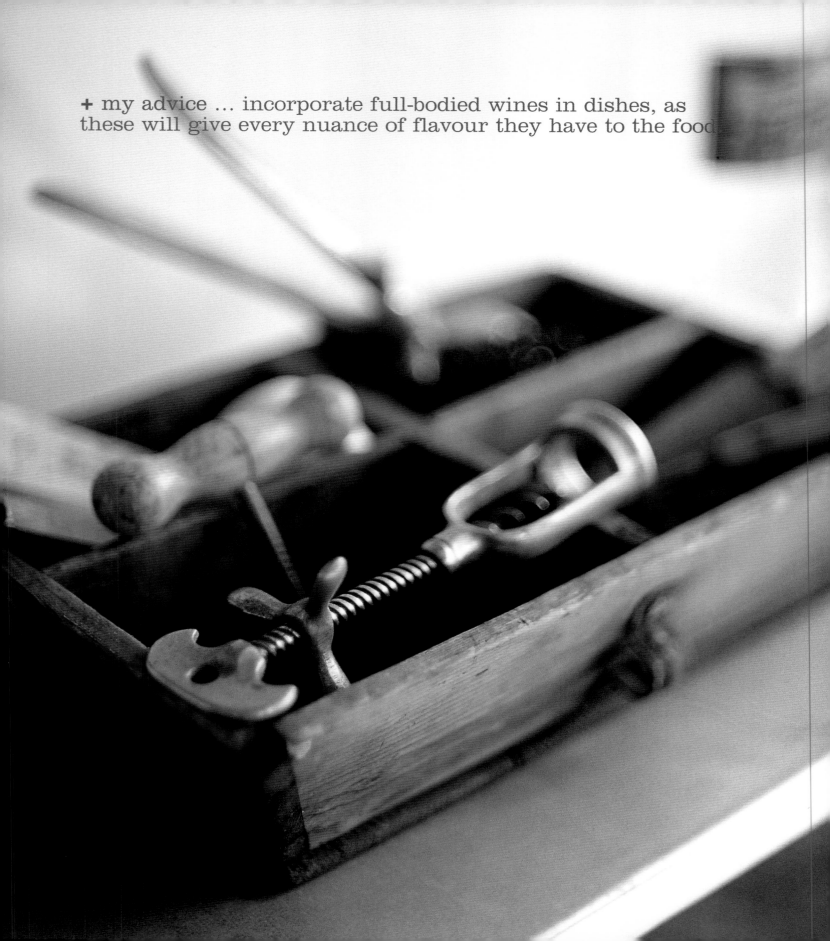

+ my advice ... incorporate full-bodied wines in dishes, as these will give every nuance of flavour they have to the food

petit coq au vin

petit coq au vin

Just for fun I've added the twist of individual-sized chickens to my version of classic coq au vin, but, of course, chicken portions are equally suitable.

olive oil

4 thickly sliced rashers rindless bacon, roughly chopped

12 pickling onions, peeled

250g button mushrooms, cleaned

sea salt and freshly ground black pepper

4 poussin (baby chickens) or 1 free-range chicken,
  cut into 8 portions

3 cloves garlic, chopped

750ml bottle dry red wine

2 bay leaves

25g softened butter

2 tablespoons plain flour

1 Heat a little oil in a flameproof casserole dish. Add bacon to brown; remove to one side. Add onions and cook for 2–3 minutes, tossing regularly, until golden; remove to one side. Add a little more oil and cook mushrooms for 3–4 minutes; remove to one side.

2 Season chickens or chicken pieces with salt and pepper and brown in batches for 1–2 minutes on each side; remove to one side.

3 Add garlic and cook for 30 seconds, then pour in the wine to deglaze the pan (see note below), and boil for 5 minutes. Add bay leaves and return bacon, onions, mushrooms and chicken to the pan. Cover pan with lid, reduce heat to a simmer and cook for 1 hour until the chicken is tender (cooking can be completed in the oven at 180°C, if preferred).

4 Remove chicken from pan and keep warm. Combine butter and flour to form a smooth paste. Bring cooking liquid to the boil and whisk in the butter/flour paste, cooking for 5 minutes until the sauce is smooth and slightly thickened. Adjust seasoning with salt and pepper if necessary. Return chicken to the sauce and serve with steamed baby potatoes and French beans.

Serves 6

+ deglaze ... is a culinary term that indicates the addition of a small amount of liquid, such as wine or stock, to a cooking pan to dissolve the flavoursome sediment from the bottom of the pan. Stir as the liquid comes to the boil to incorporate the sediment into the sauce.

fragrant vegetable curry

I enjoy serving this curry when vegetarian friends come for dinner or when I'm not feeling like eating a meaty meal. Serve lots of interesting accompaniments on the side to form a lavish feast. Try sambals such as yoghurt with grated cucumber, banana slices dipped in desiccated coconut, mango chutney, diced tomatoes and chillies, nuts and raisins.

2 tablespoons vegetable oil, such as sunflower
  or grape seed oil

2 large onions, peeled and sliced

2 tablespoons quality curry powder, medium-heat

2 cups vegetable stock

4 large carrots, peeled and cut into sticks

4 parsnips, peeled and cut into sticks

250g green beans, trimmed

1 head broccoli, cut into florets

1 cup thick plain yoghurt

sea salt and freshly ground black pepper

1/2 cup fresh coriander leaves

extra fresh chilli to serve if desired

1 Heat a large saucepan, add oil and onions and cook over a low heat for 10 minutes to soften but not colour. Add curry powder, raise the heat and cook for 1 minute, stirring constantly to toast the spice. Pour in the stock and simmer for 5 minutes.

2 Add carrot and parsnip sticks to the pan and simmer, uncovered, for 5 minutes. Add beans and broccoli and simmer for a further 5 minutes. Vegetables should be tender and the liquid reduced by half.

3 Remove pan from the heat, stir in yoghurt and season with salt and pepper to taste. Once the yoghurt has been added, do not allow the mixture to boil or it will curdle.

4 Scatter with coriander leaves and serve with steamed fragrant rice, such as basmati or jasmine rice, and fresh chilli on the side if desired.

Serves 4

+ good idea ... a good vegetable stock forms an important flavour base for many vegetarian recipes. To make this stock, roughly chop plenty of non-starchy vegetables such as carrots, onions, leeks and celery and cook in a large saucepan with a little olive oil over a moderate heat for 15 minutes to brown. Add a bay leaf, some peppercorns and 2 litres of cold water. Bring to the boil, then simmer for 45 minutes to reduce by a third. Strain to remove vegetables and skim oil from surface. Use as recipe requires. Like other stocks, vegetable stock can be frozen for future use.

osso buco al pomodoro with milanese-style risotto

This Italian recipe of long-cooked veal shanks in a saturated tomato sauce is traditionally served with a Milanese saffron-infused risotto.

12 4cm thick slices of veal hind shank
seasoned flour to dust (flour with salt and pepper added)
4 tablespoons olive oil
50g butter
1 large onion, finely diced
1 carrot, finely diced
2 sticks celery, finely diced
3 cloves garlic, crushed
1½ cups dry white wine
1½ cups beef stock
400g can peeled Italian tomatoes, crushed
3 bay leaves
1 tablespoon chopped Italian parsley
sea salt and freshly ground black pepper

1 Preheat oven to 180°C. Heat a heavy-based pan. Toss meat in seasoned flour to coat. Add oil to pan and brown meat thoroughly, then place in an ovenproof casserole.
2 Add butter, onion, carrot, celery and garlic to the pan. Reduce the heat and cook until softened but not browned. Add the wine over heat to deglaze the pan (see page 88).
3 Add the stock, tomatoes and bay leaves. Bring to the boil and pour over meat in casserole. Cover tightly and place in oven for 2 hours, turning the meat once during cooking. The meat should be tender and a dense sauce formed. Add a little more stock if sauce evaporates too quickly during cooking.
4 Add parsley (or gremalada, see below) at end of cooking time and adjust seasoning of sauce with salt and pepper to taste. Serve with Milanese-style risotto.

Serves 6

milanese-style risotto

5 cups quality chicken stock
3–4 tablespoons extra virgin olive oil
1 large onion, finely diced
2 cups Italian risotto rice, such as Carnaroli, Vialone nano or Arborio
½ teaspoon saffron threads dissolved in ¼ cup boiling water
½ cup grated fresh Parmesan
sea salt and freshly ground black pepper

1 Place stock in a small saucepan and bring to the boil, then turn down the heat to a simmer.
2 Heat a large heavy-based saucepan, add oil and onion and cook over a medium heat for 5 minutes until onion is softened but not coloured. Add risotto rice, stirring over heat for 2 minutes to toast but not brown.
3 Add a ladleful of hot stock to the same pan and stir with a wooden spoon until all the stock is absorbed. Repeat this process, adding stock by the ladleful until all the stock is absorbed, the mixture is moist and creamy and the rice is tender to the bite or 'al dente' (this takes 15–20 minutes).
4 Remove from the heat, stir in the dissolved saffron and Parmesan. Season with salt and pepper to taste. Cover pan and leave for 5 minutes to steam and finish cooking.

Serves 6

+ al dente ... translates to mean 'to the tooth'. This term is usually used to describe pasta or rice that has been brought to the stage of being cooked through while still 'firm to the bite'.

+ serving suggestion ... gremalada is a traditional addition to osso buco. Combine the finely grated zest of 1 lemon with finely chopped cloves of garlic and ¼ cup chopped fresh parsley. Sprinkle over osso buco at the end of cooking time to add fragrance.

sun-dried tomato and olive-coated rack of lamb

This is a divine coating for rack of lamb. Get your butcher to trim the lamb racks for ease of preparation. Figure on one rack serving two people unless they have large appetites.

½ cup Italian parsley, chopped
½ cup finely chopped sun-dried tomatoes
½ cup chopped pitted Kalamata olives
1 tablespoon wholegrain mustard
2 whole racks of lamb, trimmed and halved
sea salt and freshly ground black pepper
1 egg, lightly beaten
olive oil

1 Preheat oven to 200°C. Combine parsley, sun-dried tomatoes, olives and mustard in a bowl; set aside. Season lamb racks with salt and pepper. Beat egg in a bowl.
2 Dip lamb racks in beaten egg, then press chopped sun-dried tomato mixture firmly onto meat. Place racks in a low-sided roasting dish and drizzle with olive oil.
3 Roast lamb for 20 minutes for medium-rare. Remove to rest and keep warm for 10 minutes before serving. Serve half a rack per person.

Serves 4

+ serving suggestion ... I recommend serving this lamb with any of the following accompaniments: crispy roast potatoes, celeriac mash, creamed leeks, sweet potato gratin or a purée of white beans.

+ my favourite ... frying pan is a skillet because of its versatility. Skillets are solid, ovenproof steel pans that can be moved from the stove top to the oven - to brown foods first then complete their cooking in the oven. Skillets are also excellent for toasting small amounts of nuts, seeds or spices, and for cooking meals for one.

roast beef with merlot mushroom sauce

As a rule of thumb, and to provide a flavour link, it's a good idea to serve the same wine used in cooking the dish with the meal.

750g eye fillet of beef, at room temperature, trimmed

1 tablespoon Dijon mustard

sea salt and freshly ground black pepper

1 tablespoon olive oil

250g field mushrooms, sliced

1 cup reduced beef stock

2 cups merlot

1 teaspoon butter, softened

1 teaspoon flour

1 Preheat oven to 225°C. Heat a pan and brown beef on all sides. Remove beef and smear with Dijon mustard and season with salt and pepper. Place beef in an oven pan and bake for 20 minutes to cook to medium-rare. Remove to rest and keep warm for 10 minutes before carving.
2 Add oil and mushrooms to the first pan and cook gently for 2 minutes. Add beef stock and merlot, bring to the boil, then simmer to reduce to a sauce consistency.
3 Blend butter and flour to a paste and whisk into sauce to thicken if necessary. Season with salt and pepper to taste.
4 Thickly slice beef and serve with sauce.

Serves 4

+ serving suggestion ... start a menu that features this robust dish as a main with something light and bright, such as prawn rice paper rolls (see page 62) or scallop and courgette salad (see page 64).

pork fillet wrapped in pears and bacon

For an interactive evening, leave plating up to restaurant chefs and serve food casually on large platters for guests to help themselves.

2 large pork fillets (approx. 400g each), trimmed

2 pears, quartered and cores removed, sliced

sea salt and freshly ground black pepper

10 rindless rashers bacon

2–3 tablespoons olive oil

1 Preheat oven to 220°C. Lay one pork fillet on a board. Arrange half the slices of pear to cover this fillet. Season well with salt and pepper. Lay the second fillet over the pears, matching the thin end of one fillet with the thick end of the other so you end up with an even-sized piece.
2 Wrap the bacon rashers end to end around the combined pork fillets to bind together, tucking slices of pear between folds. Place in a low-sided oven pan, drizzle with olive oil and season with salt and pepper.
3 Bake for 35 minutes. Remove to rest and keep warm, then thickly slice to serve drizzled with juices from the pan.
4 Serve with cooked Puy lentils and steamed spinach.

Serves 6

+ serving suggestion ... simply simmer Puy lentils for 20 minutes in boiling water, drain well, season with salt and pepper and toss with a crushed clove of garlic or two and a good drizzle of extra virgin olive oil.

05.just d

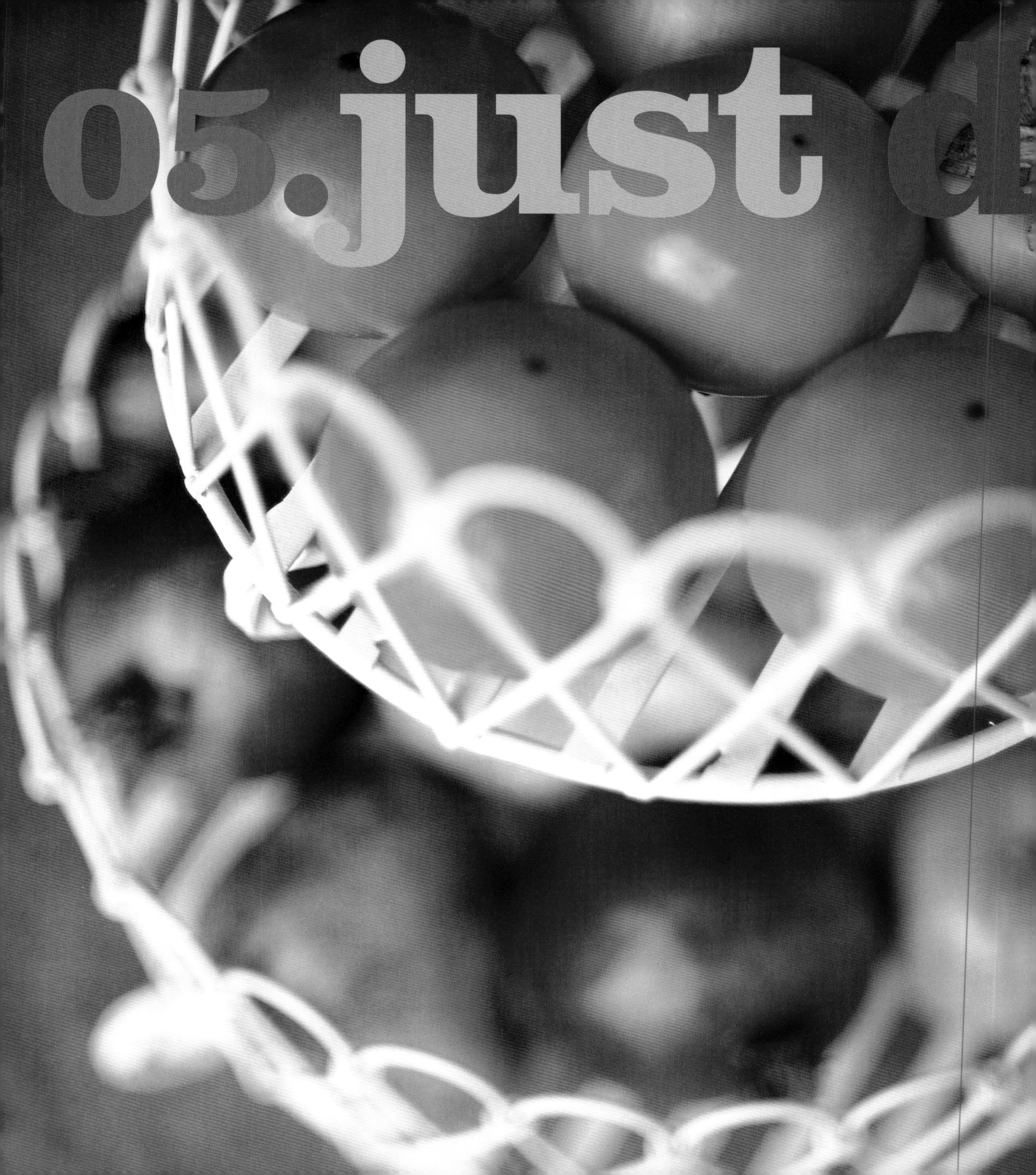

esserts

Sweet heaven by the spoonful.
Dreamy home-made delights with
lashings of cream on the side.
Impossible to resist confections
enjoyed at home with friends.

dark chocolate pots

dark chocolate pots

This memorable recipe was given to me a long time ago by the grandmother of some dear friends. I always remember Granny Arbuthnott when I make this timeless dessert.

1 cup cream
125g dark chocolate, chopped
2 egg yolks

1 Heat cream in a saucepan but do not allow to boil. Place chocolate in a bowl and pour on hot cream and leave for a few minutes to melt. Whisk together until smooth.
2 Whisk in egg yolks. Pour into 4 serving pots and refrigerate for at least 4 hours or until set.

Serves 4

+ my advice ... to ensure quick, even melting, roughly chop chocolate into small pieces before applying heat.

self-saucing chocolate hazelnut pudding

Chocolate! Few can resist this mysterious substance that for centuries has been deemed to have the various powers of a magical elixir, addictive stimulant and possible aphrodisiac.

125g butter, softened
$1/2$ cup caster sugar
2 eggs
$1/4$ cup ground toasted hazelnuts
$1/2$ cup self-raising flour
2 tablespoons Dutch process cocoa powder
$2/3$ cup brown sugar, tightly packed
3 tablespoons Dutch process cocoa powder
$1^1/4$ cups boiling water
icing sugar to dust

1 Preheat oven to 170°C. Cream butter and sugar until pale, then beat in eggs. Fold in ground hazelnuts and sifted flour and cocoa.
2 Divide chocolate pudding mixture evenly into 4 individual ovenproof dishes.
3 In a jug combine brown sugar, second measure of cocoa and boiling water. Divide by four, pouring liquid over pudding mix.
4 Bake for 25 minutes. The mixture will invert and form a chocolate sauce topped with sponge. Serve hot, dusted with icing sugar.

Serves 4

chocolate swirl sliver cake

Eating this sliver cake will remain with you as one of those died-and-gone-to-heaven experiences.

250g cream cheese, softened to room temperature

⅔ cup sugar

1 large egg

1 teaspoon pure vanilla extract

chocolate batter

150g butter, roughly cubed

300g quality dark chocolate, roughly chopped

3 large eggs

⅓ cup sugar

1 tablespoon espresso coffee

pinch salt

1 Preheat oven to fan-bake 150°C. Grease and line a 22cm springform cake tin with non-stick baking paper.

2 Place the softened cream cheese and sugar in a bowl and beat with an electric mixer until smooth. Add egg and vanilla and beat to combine. Remove to one side.

3 To make the batter, place the butter and chocolate in a medium-sized bowl and gently melt over a saucepan of simmering water, or microwave. Stir until smooth and set aside to cool a little.

4 Place the eggs, sugar, espresso and salt in another bowl and whisk with an electric mixer for 5 minutes or until very thick and pale. Gradually add the melted chocolate while continuing to whisk the mixture until combined.

5 Pour the chocolate batter into the prepared cake tin. Dollop big spoonfuls of the cream cheese mixture over the surface. Push the tip of a blunt knife deep in the batter and swirl it around to form marble patterns on the surface. Knock the cake tin with your hand to settle the batters.

6 Bake for 45 minutes or until a skewer inserted comes out sticky but not liquid coated. Leave to cool in the cake tin. When cool, carefully remove cake from tin and discard baking paper. This dessert cake lasts well if stored in the fridge.

Serves 16

+ my advice ... use a hot knife to cut this cake, wiping the blade clean between slices, and serve cut in slivers, as it is very rich.

+ my favourite ... electric mixer is a Kenwood, which is sturdy and incredibly reliable. I've had a commercial-sized Kenwood for many, many years and it's still going strong.

macadamia steamed puddings with caramel sauce

This moist and sticky caramel-flavoured, nutty pudding is perfect for a cool winter's night.

140g macadamia nuts, toasted and roughly chopped
200g butter, softened
$1^1/2$ cups caster sugar
4 eggs
3 tablespoons dark rum
$1^1/2$ cups plain flour
pinch salt
$1/2$ teaspoon baking soda
$1^1/2$ teaspoons baking powder

1 Butter 8 1-cup capacity moulds and 8 circles of baking paper cut to fit tops of moulds. Place a tablespoonful of macadamia nuts in the bottom of each mould. Preheat oven to 175°C on fan bake.
2 Place butter and sugar in a bowl and beat until smooth and creamy. Beat in eggs. Stir in rum and remaining nuts. Fold in sifted dry ingredients. Spoon mixture over macadamias to three-quarter fill moulds. Cover with buttered paper circles. Tightly cover each pudding with a piece of foil.
3 Place in a deep-sided oven pan and pour in boiling water to come half-way up the sides of the moulds. Cover pan completely with a large sheet of foil. Bake for 45 minutes. Cool a little before unmoulding. Serve with caramel sauce (see note opposite).

Serves 8

fig and ginger puddings

$1/2$ cup golden syrup
$1/4$ cup water
40g butter
$1/4$ cup tightly packed brown sugar
1 cup plain flour
1 teaspoon each ground cinnamon and ginger
$1/4$ teaspoon each ground cloves and nutmeg
$1/4$ teaspoon sea salt
$1/2$ teaspoon baking soda
4 fresh figs, slit in quarters through stem end
  leaving base intact

1 Preheat oven to 170°C. Grease 4 1-cup capacity, ovenproof, pudding bowls or ramekins.
2 Combine golden syrup, water, butter and brown sugar in a saucepan. Heat gently just until butter melts and sugar has dissolved. Remove from the heat to cool to room temperature.
3 Sift dry ingredients into a bowl. Stir golden syrup mixture into dry ingredients and mix to form a smooth batter.
4 Divide between prepared pudding bowls. Place a fig in the centre of each. Bake for 30–40 minutes or until a skewer inserted in cake mixture comes out moist but clean. Serve with caramel sauce on the side (see below).

Serves 4

+ how to make ... caramel sauce.
Combine 100g butter, $1/2$ cup cream, 1 cup tightly packed brown sugar and 1 teaspoon vanilla extract in a saucepan. Cook over a gentle heat until butter melts and sugar has dissolved. Boil for 2 minutes until mixture is syrupy. Serve hot or cold as preferred.

+ how to make ... chocolate ganache. Combine ½ cup chopped dark chocolate and ½ cup cream in a bowl and gently melt over a pan of steaming water, or microwave in short bursts. Stir to form a smooth sauce. Cool a little so that the ganache thickens, then spoon over desserts.

espresso and chocolate croissant pudding cakes

The beauty of using buttery croissants in these bread and butter pudding cakes is that you don't have to butter the bread!

8 day-old croissants

200g quality dark chocolate, chopped

½ cup raisins

½ cup brown sugar, tightly packed

4 large eggs

pinch salt

2½ cups milk

½ cup cream

1 tablespoon finely ground espresso coffee beans

100ml very strong espresso coffee

2 tablespoons brandy

2 tablespoons caster sugar

1 Preheat oven to 160°C. Grease 12 individual ¾ cup-capacity cake tins or ramekins.

2 Slice and layer croissants into prepared tins, interspersing with chocolate, raisins and sprinklings of brown sugar. Press down well.

3 Beat eggs, salt, milk, cream, ground coffee beans, espresso, brandy and sugar to combine. Pour liquid evenly over cakes and leave to rest for 30 minutes for bread to completely absorb the liquid.

4 Bake for 30 minutes. Cakes will inflate slightly when cooked, deflating again once cold. Cool a little before removing from tins. Serve warm or cold, drizzled with chocolate ganache.

Makes 12

+ zest ... is the aromatic, coloured and perfumed outer rind that sits above the white pith of the skin of citrus fruits. The zest can be removed, as required in recipes, by finely grating, or paring with a vegetable peeler, or using a special implement called a zester that creates thin strips of zest.

greek yoghurt, honey and orange syrup cake

Perfumed with zesty orange syrup, this traditional-style, semolina yoghurt cake will go straight to your heart and become a favourite.

250g butter, softened
finely grated zest and juice of 1 orange
1 cup caster sugar
3 eggs
¾ cup Greek yoghurt
½ cup semolina
2½ cups self-raising flour
Greek yoghurt to serve

1 Preheat oven to 175°C on fan bake. Grease and flour a 20cm ring tin.
2 Place butter, orange zest and sugar in a bowl and beat until pale and creamy. Beat in orange juice and eggs, then stir in Greek yoghurt. Carefully stir in semolina and sifted flour.
3 Pour into prepared tin and bake for 50 minutes or until cake tests cooked when a skewer inserted comes out clean. Turn out on a wire rack to cool.
4 Pour hot orange syrup over cooled cake (see opposite). Slice to serve with Greek yoghurt on the side.

Serves 12

orange syrup

stripped zest and juice of 3 oranges
½ cup water
½ cup liquid honey

1 Place orange zest, juice, water and honey in a saucepan and bring to the boil. Simmer for 3–5 minutes to form a syrup.

+ my advice ... for best results pour hot syrup over a cold cake and cold syrup over a hot cake. Either way, this allows the syrup to soak in without turning the cake to mush.

+ good idea ... measure ingredients on a sheet of greaseproof paper so that the scales don't need to be cleaned between measurements. Flour, for example, can be poured from the paper straight into the sieve or mixing bowl.

vanilla pear and pistachio cake

In my catering days, I often served this pear-studded, tender, fragrant cake to guests to be greeted by a round of applause!

vanilla pears

1 cup sugar

3 cups water

1 vanilla bean, split in half lengthways,
   seeds removed but kept

3 large firm pears, quartered and cored or 10 whole
   baby pears, peeled

1 Combine sugar, water, vanilla bean and seeds in a large saucepan. Bring to the boil, stirring until sugar dissolves.
2 Add pears and cook gently for 10 minutes to poach pears until just tender. Transfer pears to a bowl to cool in syrup.

pistachio cake

butter for greasing cake tin

125g butter, softened

3/4 cup caster sugar

3 eggs

2/3 cup yoghurt

2/3 cup plain flour

2/3 cup self-raising flour

1 cup ground pistachio nuts

icing sugar to dust

2 tablespoons extra ground pistachio nuts for dusting

1 Preheat oven to 160°C on fan bake. Line the base of a 26cm springform cake tin with non-stick baking paper and grease the sides of the tin with butter.
2 Combine butter and sugar in a bowl and beat with an electric mixer until creamy. Add eggs and beat well. Stir in yoghurt, then sifted flours and ground pistachios. Spread mixture in prepared cake tin and press pears into mixture. Bake for 1 hour 15 minutes or until a skewer inserted comes out clean.
3 Cool in tin, then remove to a serving plate. Dust cake with icing sugar and extra ground pistachio nuts.

Serves 10

+ serving suggestion ... for a more refreshing creamy accompaniment, blend equal quantities of whipped cream and yoghurt and serve dolloped on the side.

rose turkish delight trifle

Here I've given trifle a contemporary twist in more ways than one, and I am very pleased with my addition of Turkish delight to the mix.

1½ cups boysenberries or raspberries

3 tablespoons icing sugar

1 cup thick plain yoghurt

¾ cup cream, lightly whipped

1 teaspoon rose water

12 savoiardi (dry sponge fingers)

¼ cup sweet sherry

8 pieces rose-flavoured Turkish delight, roughly chopped

¼ cup rose petals to garnish (optional)

1 Place berries in a bowl, sprinkle with icing sugar and set aside for 30 minutes. Purée half the berries, strain and remove seeds, then combine the purée with remaining whole berries. Combine yoghurt, whipped cream and rose water in a bowl.

2 Break up sponge fingers, placing a few pieces in the base of 4 serving glasses. Drizzle with a little sherry to moisten. Cover with a good spoonful of yoghurt mix, some chopped Turkish delight and some of the berry mixture.

3 Repeat layers, finishing with a dollop of yoghurt mixture. Decorate with rose petals if desired.

Serves 4

+ flavour options ... trifle lends itself to many flavour variations. Go tropical by substituting mango purée for the berries, and incorporate shaved fresh coconut into the mix instead of the Turkish delight.

aperol and raspberry jelly

This is a very adult jelly dessert.

1 cup fresh raspberries

2 cups white wine

½ cup caster sugar

9 2g leaves gelatine or 6 teaspoons gelatine powder

¼ cup Aperol (or substitute Campari)

1 Purée raspberries in a food processor, then strain to remove seeds.

2 Place wine and sugar in a saucepan and bring to the boil, stirring until sugar has dissolved. Soak gelatine leaves in a bowl of cold water for 2–3 minutes to soften and add to hot mixture to dissolve, or sprinkle on gelatine powder and stir until grains have dissolved. Stir in raspberry purée and Aperol. Remove mixture to cool to room temperature.

3 Rinse 4 1-cup capacity moulds with cold water and place on a tray. Fill moulds with jelly mixture and place tray of moulds in the fridge for at least 4 hours (preferably overnight) to set.

4 To unmould jellies, release air lock and invert moulds onto serving plates. It may be necessary to shake moulds to free jellies. Serve with fresh fruit or whipped cream if desired.

Serves 4

+ good idea ... remove unmoulded jellies from the fridge about an hour before serving so that they soften – they're much more delicious this way and just melt in your mouth. You know they are ready to eat when they are lusciously 'wobbly'.

free-form cherry cheesecakes

I've taken a modern approach to cheesecake with this free-form version and created a classic without all the palaver.

amaretti bases

100g amaretti biscuits, crushed

1 Divide the crushed biscuits between 6 small glass dessert bowls or ramekins, pressing crumbs into the base of each.
2 Make filling.

filling

250g cream cheese, at room temperature
$\frac{1}{4}$ cup caster sugar
finely grated zest and juice of 1 lemon
250g mascarpone

1 Combine cream cheese and sugar in a bowl and beat with an electric mixer until creamy. Beat in lemon zest and juice, then mascarpone.
2 Spoon the mixture into the bowls to cover the crumb bases. Don't smooth the surface, but leave in a natural free-form shape.
3 Refrigerate while making topping.

topping

400g can black cherries in sugar syrup
1 tablespoon cornflour dissolved in $\frac{1}{4}$ cup water
2 tablespoons Kirsch (optional)

1 Drain the cherries from the syrup and set aside. Place the syrup in a saucepan with the dissolved cornflour and bring to the boil, stirring constantly until mixture thickens. Stir in cherries and Kirsch, and remove mixture to a bowl and refrigerate to cool.
2 Just before serving, spoon some chilled cherry topping over each cheesecake.

Serves 6

+ **substitute** ... any colourful fresh or preserved fruit for the cherries if desired. Try apricots, peaches, passionfruit, mango or a vibrant mix of berries.

limoncello mousse

limoncello mousse

I discovered this recipe many moons ago when I cooked for a French family in Geneva. The addition of Limoncello is a recent adaptation of mine, which I've decided I like even more than the original version.

finely grated zest and juice of 2 lemons
4 eggs, beaten
¾ cup caster sugar
¼ cup cold water
¼ cup Limoncello liqueur
½ cup firmly whipped cream

1 Place all ingredients except whipped cream in a saucepan. Heat gently, stirring constantly until mixture forms a custard that thickly coats the back of a spoon.
2 Transfer custard to a bowl and refrigerate until very cold, then fold through whipped cream. Place in 8 serving glasses and chill well before serving.
3 Garnish with caramelised lemon julienne (below) to serve.

Serves 8

+ how to make ... caramelised lemon julienne. Place the zest of 2 lemons cut into fine strips in a saucepan with ¾ cup water, ½ cup sugar and 2 tablespoons Limoncello liqueur. Bring to the boil, then turn down the heat and simmer until the mixture is syrupy and julienne strips are caramelised.

plum sago pudding

I love the texture of sago and it is especially appealing when suspended in a fruity sauce such as this.

1½ cups verjuice or dry white wine
¾ cup sugar
12 dark plums, stones removed and quartered
1 cup sago
½ cup sugar
¼ cup liquid cream

1 Place verjuice or wine and sugar in a saucepan and bring to the boil, stirring until sugar dissolves. Add plums and simmer for 10 minutes until soft. Remove to a bowl to cool.
2 Meanwhile, place sago and plenty of boiling water in a large saucepan and simmer for 25–30 minutes, stirring regularly until sago is transparent. Strain, discard cooking liquid and place sago in a bowl. Stir the second measure of sugar and half the cooked plums into the sago. Refrigerate to cool.
3 Stir cream into cold sago and divide this mixture between 6 glasses. Spoon remaining plums over sago mixture. Serve with extra whipped cream if desired.

Serves 6

+ sago ... is made from a starch obtained from the inner trunk of sago palms. When ground, washed and dried, it forms small pallets. Sago swells and becomes transparent when cooked, and is used to make puddings. It can also be used to thicken soups and stews.

burnt sugar tarts

I first ate crème brûlée in a tart-form in a quaint little patisserie in Paris. I became hooked on this concept and the first thing I did when I returned home was to recreate this taste sensation. Try it, you won't be disappointed!

sweet pastry

½ cup caster sugar
200g butter, softened
1 egg
2 cups plain flour
pinch salt

1 Place sugar, butter and egg in a bowl and beat to just combine. Stir in flour and salt to form a dough. Turn out on a floured work surface and lightly knead to bring together.
2 Wrap in plastic wrap and chill for 30 minutes before using as recipe directs.

vanilla custard

1 vanilla bean
1 cup cream
½ cup milk
2 tablespoons caster sugar
3 egg yolks
demerara sugar to brulée

1 Roll out pastry to 3mm thick and use to line 6 10cm individual tart tins. Prick bases with a fork and chill for 30 minutes.
2 Preheat oven to 190°C. Line pastry with non-stick baking paper or foil and fill with baking weights such as dried beans. Bake for 10 minutes. Remove paper and weights and return cases to the oven for another 5 minutes to dry pastry. Decrease oven temperature to 140°C.
3 Cut vanilla bean in half lengthways and scrape out the seeds. Combine bean and seeds with cream and milk in a saucepan. Bring to the boil, then remove from the heat for 10 minutes for vanilla to infuse.
4 In a bowl beat caster sugar and egg yolks together until pale. Strain cream mixture and pour onto yolks, then whisk to combine.
5 Return mixture to a clean saucepan. Cook over a gentle heat, stirring constantly until mixture forms a custard thick enough to coat the back of a spoon. Do not allow to boil or the custard will curdle. Pour custard into pastry cases. Bake for 15 minutes or until custard is just set. Remove to cool.
6 Just before serving dust top of custard with demerara sugar. Caramelise with a brlûée torch or quickly under a hot grill.

Makes 6

+ my favourite … rolling pin is a French-style rolling pin, the one with no handles that is specifically shaped for pastry work. The advantage is that this type of rolling pin is extra long and therefore leaves no indentation marks in the pastry.

vanilla pannacotta with pineapple and passionfruit salad

This is truly and deeply delicious! *Panna* means cream, *cotta* means cooked, so essentially this is a dessert of cooked cream (though I've lightened my version by replacing some cream with milk).

1 cup milk

2½ cups cream

¼ cup sugar

1 vanilla bean (see note below)

3 2g leaves gelatine or 4 teaspoons gelatine powder

1 Place milk, 2 cups of measured cream, sugar and vanilla bean and seeds in a saucepan and bring to the boil, stirring regularly. Gently simmer for 8–10 minutes, then remove vanilla bean.

2 Soak gelatine leaves in cold water to soften, then squeeze to remove excess water. Or, dissolve gelatine powder in ¼ cup water in a small ramekin, then heat ramekin in a microwave or double boiler until it becomes liquid. Whisk either gelatine option into hot cream mixture until incorporated. Set aside to cool.

3 Lightly whip remaining ½ cup of cream and fold into cooled mixture. Pour into 6 lightly oiled, ¾-cup capacity moulds or small teacups. Refrigerate for at least 4 hours (preferably overnight) to set.

4 To serve, dip moulds in boiling water for a few seconds. Invert onto plates and shake to turn out. Drizzle with pineapple and passionfruit salad.

pineapple and passionfruit salad

½ fresh pineapple, peeled

½ cup passionfruit pulp (fresh or preserved)

1 Finely dice the pineapple flesh and mix with the passionfruit pulp.

Serves 6

+ vanilla beans ... are the slender, aromatic seedpods from a tropical climbing plant of the orchid family. To remove the flavoursome edible seeds, vanilla beans need to be split in half lengthways and the tiny seeds scraped out with the tip of a knife. The pods are too tough to eat but can be infused in liquids (for example, milk or cream) or in dry goods (for example, sugar or rice) to impart their flavour.

06. late suppers

Dramatically simple creations. Honest ingredients combined to provide succour. Curl up by the fireside after the theatre or movies. Enjoy a restorative meal.

creole gumbo

The secret of a good gumbo lies in the quality of the stock and also in taking the roux to the right colour and strength of flavour. Okra is a green vegetable that acts to thicken the gumbo and is used in many other Creole dishes.

4 tablespoons vegetable oil

3 tablespoons plain flour

5 cups quality chicken stock

1 onion, peeled and diced

2 sticks celery, diced

1 green pepper, seeds removed, diced

1 cup okra, thickly sliced

400g can chopped tomatoes

1 green chilli, thinly sliced

2 bay leaves

1 teaspoon chopped fresh thyme

2 tablespoons chopped fresh parsley

sea salt and freshly ground black pepper

1½ cups long-grain rice, cooked to serve

1 Heat the oil in a large, heavy-based saucepan. Add the flour and cook over a gentle heat, stirring constantly until the flour darkens to a deep tan colour. Remove from the heat.

2 Add the stock gradually, stirring to combine. Return to the heat and bring to the boil. Add the prepared vegetables, bay leaves and thyme and simmer for 1 hour.

3 Finally, add the parsley and season with salt and pepper to taste. Serve ladled over bowls of long-grain rice.

Serves 6

+ my advice ... seafood, bacon, spicy sausage or chicken can be added and still produce an authentic gumbo. If adding chicken, do so after 40 minutes, allowing 20 minutes to simmer. If adding seafood, do so 5–10 minutes before end of cooking time.

artichoke and bacon strata

A strata is basically a savoury bread pudding flavoured with any combination of ingredients. The strata becomes fluffier in texture the longer the bread layers are left to absorb the liquid ingredients.

5 slices day-old bread, crusts removed, cut into 1cm cubes

4 rindless rashers bacon, roughly chopped and cooked

¾ cup artichoke hearts

3 spring onions, chopped

1 red pepper, seeds removed, finely diced

100g goats' cheese or feta, crumbled

2 tablespoons chopped fresh oregano

3 large eggs

1 teaspoon Dijon mustard

1¼ cups milk

¼ cup cream

sea salt and freshly ground black pepper

1 Place half the bread in a greased, deep-sided, 2-litre-capacity baking dish. Layer half the bacon, artichokes, spring onions, red pepper, cheese and oregano over bread. Top with remaining bread cubes and then remaining layer of bacon, etc.

2 In a large bowl whisk eggs with mustard, milk and cream. Season with salt and pepper and pour over strata. Press the bread down to be sure that the strata is fully covered. Set aside for at least 30 minutes for bread to fully absorb the liquid.

3 Preheat oven to 170°C. Bake uncovered for 40–50 minutes until set and golden brown. Cover with foil half-way through cooking if the surface becomes too brown. The strata will puff up during cooking and deflate once removed from the oven. Let stand for 10 minutes before serving.

Serves 8

+ substitute ... day-old croissants or brioches work well in place of the bread. For variety replace the bacon, artichoke and feta with a combination of mushrooms, blue cheese and thyme, or smoked fish, capers and dill.

mushroom goulash

I've been making this, my version of mushroom goulash, for the longest time and find it a very comforting dish. I recommend finding and adding the smoked paprika for superior taste.

olive oil

2 large onions, peeled and finely chopped

3 cloves garlic, chopped

1 red pepper, seeds removed, finely diced

250g field mushrooms, thickly sliced

250g button mushrooms, halved

2 teaspoons bittersweet Spanish smoked paprika

1 tablespoon plain flour

1 cup tomato purée

1 cup sour cream

sea salt and freshly ground black pepper

2 tablespoons chopped fresh parsley

1 Heat a large frying pan, add 2–3 tablespoons olive oil, onions, garlic and pepper and cook over a medium heat for 10 minutes until softened but not coloured; remove to one side. In the same pan, raise the heat, add mushrooms and cook for 5 minutes to brown, tossing regularly; remove to one side.

2 Add 2 tablespoons more oil to the pan along with the paprika and flour and mix to form a smooth paste. Remove from the heat and stir in the tomato purée to form a smooth sauce. Bring back to the boil, stirring until sauce thickens.

3 Add sour cream and stir to combine but do not boil once sour cream has been added or mixture may curdle.

4 Return all the vegetables to the pan, stirring to combine. Season with salt and pepper to taste. Serve scattered with parsley.

Serves 4

+ **serving suggestion** ... I find that fettuccine, steamed fragrant rice or creamy mashed potato make great accompaniments to this dish. Serve a green vegetable such as spinach, broccoli or Brussels sprouts on the side.

baked penne, beef and mushroom layers

I guess you could say that this is the time-poor-yet-clever person's lasagne! While minus a bit of layering, this dish certainly doesn't lack flavour.

olive oil

500g beef mince

1 onion, peeled and diced

250g button mushrooms, halved

400g can chopped tomatoes

3 tablespoons chopped fresh herbs (parsley, oregano, and thyme)

sea salt and freshly ground black pepper

250g penne pasta

2 cups sour cream

2 egg yolks

1/2 cup freshly grated Parmesan

1 Heat a large pan, add a little oil and brown beef mince for 5–8 minutes, stirring regularly to break up any lumps. Remove from pan to one side.

2 Add a little more oil to the pan and gently cook onion and mushrooms. Stir in tomatoes and cooked mince, and simmer for 5 minutes. Add herbs and season with salt and pepper to taste. Pour cooked mince into the base of a deep-sided casserole dish.

3 Preheat oven to 180°C. Cook pasta in a large saucepan of boiling salted water for 10 minutes, or according to packet instructions, until just tender to the bite. Drain and layer pasta on top of mince.

4 Blend sour cream with egg yolks and season with salt and pepper. Spread this mixture evenly over pasta. Sprinkle with grated Parmesan and bake for 20–30 minutes until golden brown.

Serves 4

+ **my advice** ... buy quality pasta. Good dried pasta holds sauces well, has a higher yield per kilo, retains more texture, bite and mouth-appeal and, most importantly, just tastes better than the everyday stuff.

+ my advice ... to retain the full flavour of mushrooms, it is best not to wash or peel them. Modern mushrooms are generally very clean, so simply wipe them with a damp cloth to remove any dirt if necessary.

macadamia chicken and lentil salad

Once again, Spanish smoked paprika comes to the foreground in flavouring this simple salad.

1 cup green Puy lentils (see note opposite)

2 cloves garlic, crushed

3 tablespoons aged balsamic vinegar

1/4 cup extra virgin olive oil

4 skinless chicken breasts

sea salt and freshly ground black pepper

olive oil for frying

1/2 cup toasted macadamia nuts

1 teaspoon sweet Spanish smoked paprika

50g baby rocket or baby lettuce leaves

1/2 cup caper berries, sliced

1 Place lentils in a saucepan with plenty of cold water and bring to the boil. Turn down the heat and simmer for 20 minutes until lentils are just tender. Drain well, toss with crushed garlic, balsamic vinegar and extra virgin olive oil, and set aside to cool.

2 Lay each chicken breast flat and slice horizontally into 4 pieces about the size of a chicken tenderloin. Season chicken with salt and pepper. Heat a non-stick frying pan, add a little oil and cook chicken pieces in batches for 2–3 minutes on each side to brown and cook through. Remove to one side.

3 Grind macadamia nuts in a food mill with smoked paprika.

4 Arrange chicken on a bed of lentils. Dust chicken with ground macadamia nuts and paprika mixture. Scatter with rocket leaves and sliced caper berries to serve.

Serves 4

+ substitute ... the smoked paprika is essential, however, any other type of nut could be exchanged for the macadamias; try cashews, Brazil nuts, walnuts or almonds. I would steer away from peanuts, as the flavour would not work with the others in this dish.

+ Puy lentils ... are green lentils grown around Le-Puy-en-Velay in France. These lentils are of such quality that they do not need cleaning or soaking before cooking; they also take less time to cook than other varieties. Puy lentils remain slightly crisp when cooked and have a wonderful spicy, nutty flavour.

chicken and vegetables with fragrant peanut sauce

With an interplay of aromatic, toasty flavours, this dish makes the perfect fireside supper.

1 cup raw peanuts

3cm piece ginger, peeled and chopped

3 tablespoons light soy sauce

2 tablespoons tomato paste

1 teaspoon cinnamon

1/2 teaspoon ground cardamom

3 cups chicken stock

3 large skinless chicken breasts, cut into 2cm thick strips

250g green beans, trimmed

4 zucchini, sliced

1 red pepper, seeds removed, cut into strips

sea salt and freshly ground black pepper

1/4 cup chopped fresh coriander or parsley

1 Heat oven to 180°C. Place peanuts in an oven pan and roast for 15 minutes until golden brown. Remove to cool.
2 Place cold peanuts, ginger, soy sauce, tomato paste, cinnamon and cardamom in the bowl of a food processor and grind to a paste. Blend in chicken stock. Transfer mixture to a saucepan and bring to the boil, then simmer for 5 minutes.
3 Add chicken and vegetables and simmer gently for 5–8 minutes to cook. Adjust seasoning with salt and pepper to taste. Serve scattered with chopped coriander or parsley.

Serves 4

chicken schnitzel with cherry tomato and rocket sauce

Cherry tomatoes combined with tomato juice are quite a different base from which to make a tomato sauce. This results in a dish that explodes with flavour as each tiny tomato bursts.

4 chicken schnitzels (chicken breasts pounded flat)

sea salt and freshly ground black pepper

olive oil

1 1/2 cups red cherry tomatoes

3 cloves garlic, crushed

2 cups tomato juice

100g rocket leaves

1 Season chicken with salt and pepper. Heat a non-stick frying pan with a little oil and panfry chicken schnitzels in batches for 3–4 minutes on each side to brown and cook through. Remove to a serving plate and keep warm while preparing the sauce.
2 Add a little more oil to the pan plus the cherry tomatoes and garlic and stir-fry for 1–2 minutes over a medium heat, tossing regularly. Add the tomato juice and simmer for 5 minutes. Lastly, add the rocket to wilt and adjust seasoning with salt and pepper to taste. Pour sauce over prepared chicken.

Serves 4

+ shortcut ... when peeling large quantities of garlic or if the skin is particularly tight, blanch whole cloves in boiling water for 1 minute, then plunge into cold water. This removes any stickiness and the skins will simply slip off.

salmon rissoles with pickled fennel and cucumber

What I find works when I'm planning a late supper is to pickle the vegetables in the morning and form the salmon rissoles, then refrigerate everything until you're ready to eat. All this dish requires at suppertime is a quick dip in a hot pan.

pickled fennel and cucumber

1/2 cup white wine vinegar

1/4 cup caster sugar

1 teaspoon salt

1 fennel bulb, trimmed

1/2 telegraph cucumber, halved lengthways, seeds removed

1 small red chilli, seeds removed, finely chopped

1 Combine vinegar, sugar and salt in a bowl and stir until sugar dissolves.
2 Thinly slice fennel and cucumber on the diagonal and add to pickling liquid. Cover and refrigerate for at least 30 minutes or preferably overnight.

salmon rissoles

600g fresh salmon fillet, skin and pin bones removed (see page 149)

2 spring onions, very finely chopped

1/3 cup chopped fresh coriander

1 small chilli, seeds removed, very finely chopped

sea salt and freshly ground black pepper

vegetable oil for frying

1 Very finely chop the salmon, place in a bowl and combine with remaining ingredients (except oil). Season well with salt and pepper.
2 With wet hands (dip hands in a bowl of cold water from time to time) form mixture into 8 round patties and place these on a tray.
3 Heat a non-stick frying pan, add a little oil and fry rissoles for 2–3 minutes on each side over a medium heat. Remove rissoles to drain on paper towels. Serve 2 per person, topped with pickled fennel and cucumber.

Serves 4

+ **visual impact** ... when arranging a dish, aim to centralise the ingredients on the plate by piling or stacking them up attractively.

angel hair pasta with smoked tuna and lemon

This dish would also work well as a starter, served in small nests of noodles on individual plates.

350g angel hair pasta (spaghettini or tagliolini)

1/4 cup olive oil

3 cloves garlic, chopped

1/2 cup cream

zest and juice of 1 lemon

300g smoked fish, such as tuna or trout, flaked

1/2 cup torn fresh basil leaves

sea salt and freshly ground black pepper

1 Cook pasta in a large saucepan of boiling salted water for 2–3 minutes, or according to packet instructions, until al dente. Drain in a colander.

2 Meanwhile, heat oil in a large saucepan, add garlic and cook for 30 seconds over a medium heat. Add cream, lemon zest, juice, tuna and basil and simmer for 1–2 minutes to heat.

3 Toss hot drained pasta in hot sauce. Season with salt and pepper to taste and serve immediately.

Serves 4

+ my advice ... when cooking pasta, there is no need to add oil to the cooking water, but it is wise to separate the pieces with an initial stirring.

tuna, feta, rocket and pasta salad

This would be the ultimate dish to return home to after a movie or the theatre. Throw it all together (except the rocket, as this wilts) before you depart and leave for the flavours to heighten – a veritable feast awaits your return.

300g pasta shapes, such as cavatelli, macaroni, fuselli

150g green beans, trimmed and cooked

1 red pepper, seeds removed

370g canned quality tuna, drained and flaked

150g feta cheese, cubed

150g baby rocket leaves

2 cloves garlic, peeled and chopped

sea salt and freshly ground black pepper

1/4 cup quality balsamic vinegar

1/4 cup extra virgin olive oil

1 Cook pasta in a large saucepan of boiling salted water for 10 minutes, or according to packet instructions, until just tender to the bite. Drain and run under cold water to cool. Drain well and toss with a little olive oil to prevent sticking.

2 Slice green beans and red pepper and toss with cold pasta, flaked tuna, feta, rocket leaves and garlic. Season with salt and pepper to taste.

3 Drizzle with balsamic vinegar and olive oil, toss well and serve.

Serves 4

+ my advice ... as a rule of thumb, short pasta shapes are easy to eat with chunky sauces where the ingredients are of a similar size to the pasta. Smooth, wet sauces work well with long styles of pasta, such as spaghetti or fettuccine.

+ my advice ... to peel beetroot with ease, cook beetroot whole, then drain well. Set aside until cool enough to handle then the skins will simply slip off in your hands. This is the best method because if beetroot are peeled before cooking they will bleed their colour and goodness into the cooking water.

warm chorizo, beetroot and feta salad

Warm autumnal colours and flavours combine in this salad that is light and yet satisfying.

500g baby beetroot, scrubbed
4 chorizo, sliced diagonally 1cm thick
¼ cup extra virgin olive oil
150g baby rocket
150g feta, crumbled
2–3 tablespoons Spanish sherry vinegar
sea salt and freshly ground black pepper

1 Trim beetroot, reserving any baby leaves for the salad. Cook beetroot whole in plenty of boiling water for about 10 minutes or until tender. Drain and remove to a bowl to cool a little.
2 Heat a frying pan, add a little oil and brown chorizo slices on both sides. Remove to drain on paper towels.
3 Arrange beetroot, chorizo, rocket and baby beetroot leaves on a serving platter and scatter with crumbled feta. Drizzle with sherry vinegar and extra virgin olive oil, and season with salt and pepper. Serve warm with some crusty bread if desired.

Serves 4

paprika pork with potatoes and spinach

Smoked Spanish paprika adds a pungent smoky taste to this dish. Look for it at delis and specialty food stores.

olive oil

6 rindless rashers bacon, roughly chopped

1 red onion, sliced

600g pork rump steaks, thickly sliced

1 tablespoon sweet or bittersweet smoked Spanish paprika

2 tablespoons plain flour

1/2 cup dry white wine

400g can chopped tomatoes

3 large waxy potatoes, peeled and quartered

sea salt and freshly ground black pepper

150g baby spinach leaves

1 Heat a large saucepan, add oil and bacon to brown, then add onion and cook gently for 5 minutes. Remove to one side. Add pork to the same pan in batches to brown for 1 minute on each side, with a little more oil if necessary. Remove to one side.
2 Add paprika and flour to the same pan and stir to form a smooth paste. Remove pan from heat, add wine and stir until smooth. Return bacon, onion and pork to the pan, then add tomatoes and potatoes. Cover and simmer very gently for 35–40 minutes.
3 Adjust seasoning with salt and pepper. Lastly, stir in spinach to wilt for a few minutes before serving.

Serves 4

classic seafood chowder

Often a simple dish will capture our hearts and become cherished in our culinary reminiscences – this one does it for me every time.

2 tablespoons olive oil

50g butter

1 onion, finely chopped

3 cloves garlic, crushed

1/4 cup plain flour

3 cups milk

2 cups fish or vegetable stock

1/4 cup liquid cream (optional)

750g mixed seafood, such as a selection of prawns or shrimp, scallops, mussels, sliced squid and/or cubed white-fleshed fish

3 tablespoons chopped fresh thyme or parsley

sea salt and freshly ground black pepper

1 Heat a large saucepan, add oil and butter to melt, then add onion and garlic and cook for 5–10 minutes over a gentle heat until softened but not coloured. Stir in flour and cook for 1 minute.
2 Gradually add milk and stock, stirring constantly over heat until sauce thickens. Add cream to enrich, if desired.
3 Add selected mixed seafood and cook over a gentle heat for 5–8 minutes. Sprinkle with thyme or parsley and season with salt and pepper to taste.

Serves 6

+ serving suggestion ... serve with crusty fresh bread, or for variety, here are some different accompaniment ideas: try golden-baked small squares of puff pastry, or roughly torn ciabatta, drizzled with olive oil and baked until crisp.

 + Spanish smoked paprika ... is made from Spanish pimientos (a sweet and spicy variety of capsicum pepper) that have been smoked over oak and ground to produce a powder, which adds a distinctive smoky, spicy flavour to food. Spanish smoked paprika is quite different in taste to the more common Hungarian paprika – look for it in specialty food stores.

cinnamon hot chocolate

Good enough to enjoy as a fireside dessert!

150g quality dark chocolate, chopped
1$^1/_2$ cups milk
1 cinnamon stick

1 Melt chocolate carefully in a bowl over a double boiler, or microwave in short bursts. Heat milk and cinnamon stick together in a pan until hot but not boiling. Leave briefly for flavours to infuse, then remove cinnamon stick.
2 Pour hot milk onto melted chocolate, whisking to blend. Pour into cups to serve.

Serves 2

+ my advice ... always melt chocolate over a very gentle heat (or microwave in short bursts) to avoid the risk of it irreparably seizing or burning.

hot toddy

This hot toddy will warm you from head to toe.

6 whole cloves
pared zest and juice of 1 lemon
1 tablespoon honey
$^1/_2$ cup boiling water
$^1/_2$ cup whisky

1 Place cloves, lemon juice and honey in a jug. Pour on boiling water and stir to combine.
2 Stir in whisky, pour into cups or glasses and garnish with lemon zest.

Serves 2

+ my advice ... snuggle up on a cold evening, light the fire if you have one, or flood the house with candles, which create a remarkable amount of heat and atmosphere!

07.celeb

rations

Weave together magical dishes to celebrate special days, family and friends. Sharing food with loved ones creates happy and indelible memories.

veal with sage and caper sauce

I recommend cooking this dish for very good friends and not for new acquaintances that you're trying to impress because for the veal to remain moist and tender, it really does require last-minute cooking.

2 cloves garlic, peeled

3 tablespoons olive oil

700g (4 large) veal escalopes

sea salt and freshly ground black pepper

25g butter

4 tablespoons fresh sage leaves

1/4 cup capers, rinsed and drained

1/2 cup marsala

1 Crush garlic and mix with oil. Rub into veal and set aside until ready to cook.

2 Heat a non-stick frying pan and add a little oil. Season veal with salt and pepper and pan-fry for 2–3 minutes on each side to brown. This may need to be done in 2–3 batches. Remove to a hot serving platter.

3 Add butter to the pan to melt, then add sage leaves and cook for 30 seconds until crisp. Add capers and marsala and simmer for a few minutes to reduce by half, scraping the pan to incorporate any residue into the sauce.

4 Pour hot pan juices over veal to serve.

Serves 4

+ serving suggestion ... serve a medley of different steamed vegetables as a side dish. Slice vegetables in unexpected ways, such as cutting carrots into half moons, courgettes into ribbons, broccoli into shards, or beans into small rounds.

glazed ham

A beautifully glazed ham creates a centrepiece for any festive table. The aroma and taste provide a veritable feast for the senses.

8–9kg whole ham, cooked on the bone

1 cup orange juice

mustard and apricot glaze

1 cup apricot jam

1 cup tightly packed brown sugar

3 tablespoons wholegrain mustard

1 Preheat oven to 180°C. Run a knife around the shank end of the ham. Carefully slice under the edge of the rind at the base of the ham, then ease between the rind and the fat with your fingers and pull to gently remove the rind.

2 Using a sharp knife, score the fat in a diamond pattern with 3mm deep cuts. Place ham in an oven pan large enough to catch any glaze that will drip as it cooks. Surround ham with orange juice.

3 Combine glaze ingredients in a bowl. Smear glaze over scored fat of ham. Place ham in the oven and bake for 1 hour, basting at regular intervals until glaze has caramelised to a golden brown.

4 Sliced ham can be served hot or at room temperature.

Makes glaze for 1 whole ham to serve up to 45 people

+ how to ... store ham for up to 2 weeks. Cover surface of ham securely with a clean, damp tea towel or piece of muslin, rinsing the cloth every day to keep it moist. Do not cover with plastic wrap as this will cause the ham to sweat and deteriorate more quickly. Ham can be frozen (for up to 3 months), wrapped in paper and then securely in foil, however some moisture will be lost on thawing.

roast chicken with chestnut and apple stuffing

This is like old-fashioned stuffed chicken, yet elegantly and individually portioned. If chestnuts are hard to come by, Brazil nuts make a good substitute.

200g Italian-style fennel sausage meat, or coarse-
  textured fennel sausages removed from their casings
100g chopped chestnuts
1 apple, coarsely grated
2 tablespoons brandy
6 chicken breasts (skin on)
6 large thin slices prosciutto
olive oil
sea salt and freshly ground black pepper

1 Preheat oven to 200°C. With damp hands, remove the sausage casings if necessary and place sausage meat in a bowl with chestnuts, grated apple and brandy. Mix well to combine, then divide mixture by six.
2 Loosen the skin of the chicken breasts and stuff one portion of the mix under the skin of each chicken breast, smoothing surface to evenly distribute stuffing. Wrap each chicken breast in one slice of prosciutto.
3 Place chicken breasts in an oven pan, drizzle with a little olive oil and season with salt and pepper. Roast for 25–30 minutes until golden brown and cooked through.

Serves 6

+ serving sugestion ... side dishes should complement and enhance the main event – think of complementary flavours, colours and textural contrasts. With this chicken, I recommend serving steamed green beans topped with shavings of garlic gently fried in olive oil.

crisp duck with dried cranberry sauce

Duck breasts are particularly moist and succulent when served delightfully pink.

4 duck breasts
sea salt and freshly ground black pepper

1 Preheat oven to 190°C. With a sharp knife, score the skin of each duck breast in a diamond pattern with 3mm deep cuts. Season with salt and pepper.
2 Heat an ovenproof frying pan and place duck breasts skin-side-down. Cook over a medium heat for 5–8 minutes until the skin is golden brown and crisp. Pour off the rendered fat. Turn duck breasts and place pan in the oven. Roast for 5–8 minutes, then remove to rest and keep warm for 10 minutes before slicing and serving with hot cranberry sauce.

dried cranberry sauce

finely grated zest and juice of 1 orange
1/4 cup Cointreau or brandy
3/4 cup dried cranberries
1/2 cup cranberry sauce or redcurrant jelly

1 Combine orange zest, juice, Cointreau and dried cranberries in a bowl and leave to soak for 10 minutes for cranberries to swell.
2 Place all ingredients in a saucepan and bring to the boil. Simmer for 2–3 minutes to thicken to a pouring consistency.

Serves 4

+ good idea ... toss cooked, sliced baby potatoes in basil pesto and serve hot.

roast turkey and dried peach salad with toasted pine nut dressing

Whatever the occasion, I like to celebrate sharing food with family and friends with a decorated table, flowers, candles and pretty napkins.

250g dried peaches (or substitute dried apricots), sliced
1/4 cup muscat
2 500g single turkey breasts
sea salt and freshly ground black pepper
olive oil
1 cos lettuce or mixed baby lettuce leaves
1/4 cup toasted pine nuts
3 tablespoons snipped fresh chives

1 Combine peaches and muscat in a bowl and leave to soak for several hours or overnight.
2 Preheat oven to 190°C. Season turkey breasts with salt and pepper. Heat an ovenproof frying pan, add a little olive oil and brown turkey breasts on both side. Transfer to the oven to roast for 20–25 minutes or until juices run clear. Remove from oven to rest and cool.
3 Once cold, slice turkey thinly against the grain of the meat and place in a large salad bowl with the soaked peaches and muscat and lettuce.
4 Toss well with pine nut dressing to coat and adjust seasoning if necessary. Serve salad scattered with pine nuts and snipped chives.

toasted pine nut dressing

1/4 cup toasted pine nuts
1 teaspoon Dijon mustard
3–4 tablespoons Spanish sherry vinegar
1/3 cup extra virgin olive oil
sea salt and freshly ground black pepper

1 Blend ingredients in a food processor to form a textured dressing. Season with salt and pepper to taste and pour over salad.

Serves 4

+ visual impact ... invest in some visually impressive, big white serving platters; white is still generally the best colour as it shows off the beauty of the food.

marinated butterflied leg of lamb with pineapple salsa

For entertaining a crowd you can't go past a tender leg of lamb, which can be bought with the bone removed so all the work is done. Once opened out flat, this is termed butterflied (like the wings of a giant butterfly).

2kg leg of lamb, boned and butterflied
sea salt and freshly ground black pepper

marinade

1/4 cup white wine vinegar
1 cup pineapple juice
3 tablespoons grated fresh ginger
1/4 cup honey
1/4 cup olive oil

1 Place lamb in a deep, flat, non-metallic dish. Combine marinade ingredients and pour over lamb. Cover with plastic wrap, refrigerate and leave to marinate for several hours or preferably overnight.
2 Preheat oven to 180°C. Transfer lamb to a large oven pan, season with salt and pepper and roast for 45–55 minutes to cook lamb to medium-rare. Baste with marinade several times during cooking.
3 Remove lamb to rest and keep warm for 10 minutes before carving. Slice and serve with pineapple salsa on the side.

pineapple salsa

1 small pineapple, skin removed with a sharp knife
2 small red chillies, seeds removed, finely chopped
1/2 cup chopped fresh coriander
3 tablespoons white wine vinegar
2 tablespoons olive oil
sea salt and freshly ground black pepper

1 Finely dice pineapple flesh and mix with remaining ingredients, tossing well to combine. Season with salt and pepper to taste.

Serves 12

+ good idea ... searing meat caramelises its natural sugars, which turn brown and add depth of flavour and richness to the completed dish. This works for all meat, from a simple steak to barbecued lamb, to cubed meat for a stew.

salmon with asian-inspired dressing and green vegetable medley

This is a great dish to serve for any summer-time celebration. The Asian-inspired dressing is wonderfully fresh and fragrant and adds a certain zing to the salmon.

green vegetable medley

500g snow peas, trimmed
250g peas (fresh or frozen)
2 bunches asparagus, trimmed and halved diagonally
250g podded broad beans (fresh or frozen)
extra virgin olive oil
sea salt and freshly ground black pepper

1 Blanch snow peas, peas and asparagus in boiling salted water for 2 minutes, then drain well and refresh in ice-cold water. Drain well and place in a large bowl.
2 Blanch broad beans for 30 seconds in boiling water, then drain and refresh in ice-cold water. Peel and discard outer shell of broad beans and add beans to bowl.
3 Drizzle vegetable medley with extra virgin olive oil and season with salt and pepper to taste. Toss well to serve.

roast salmon

1kg salmon fillet, skin and pin bones removed (see note below)
sea salt and freshly ground black pepper
extra kaffir lime leaves to garnish

1 Preheat oven to 200°C. Season salmon portions with salt and pepper. Heat a non-stick frying pan, add a little oil and place salmon portions in pan skin-side-up to brown for 2 minutes.
2 Turn salmon and place in a large low-sided oven pan. Roast for 10 minutes. Arrange salmon on top of vegetables and spoon over Asian-inspired dressing.
3 Garnish with extra kaffir lime leaves.

asian-inspired dressing

2 tablespoons light soy sauce
2 tablespoons Thai fish sauce
juice of 2 limes
1/4 cup chopped fresh coriander
1 kaffir lime leaf, very finely chopped

1 Combine all ingredients in a bowl. Adjust quantities to taste to achieve a balanced taste.

Serves 6

+ how to ... remove pin bones from salmon. Run your index finger down the length of the salmon fillet to feel for the row of protruding pin-like bones. Using sterilised tweezers or specifically designed salmon-bone tweezers, securely grip the tip of each bone and pull out in the opposite direction from where the bone lies. Work down the row until no bones remain.

+ a small bunch of herbs tied together with string is called a *bouquet garni*. This herbal bundle is dangled in a soup or stew to add flavour and then easily removed by pulling the string. Typical *bouquet garni* herbs are parsley stalks, thyme and bay leaves, however rosemary, oregano or sage may sometimes be included.

PARSLEY

amazing christmas cake

This fruit cake is amazing because it contains no eggs at all – and it tastes amazing. I've had people beg me for this favourite recipe over the years – so, here it is!

225g butter, melted

1 cup hot water

1 tablespoon white wine vinegar

2 teaspoons cinnamon

1 teaspoon mixed spice

1kg dried fruit (I like an even mix of currants, raisins and sultanas)

1 can sweetened condensed milk

1 teaspoon baking soda

¼ cup sherry

1 teaspoon vanilla extract

2¼ cups self-raising flour, sifted

¼ cup whole almonds to decorate

brandy to douse

1 Place butter, hot water, vinegar, cinnamon, mixed spice and dried fruit into a large saucepan and bring to the boil, stirring regularly.

2 Remove from the heat and stir in condensed milk and baking soda. Allow to cool to room temperature.

3 Line a deep-sided 20cm round cake tin with non-stick baking paper and preheat oven to 140°C on fan bake.

4 Add sherry and vanilla to cooled mixture and stir in sifted flour. Pour into prepared cake tin and decorate top with almonds.

5 Bake for 2–2½ hours. Cool completely before removing from cake tin. Prick with a skewer and douse with brandy if desired.

Makes 1 deep-sided cake

+ my advice … Christmas fruit cakes are traditionally made in advance, laced with brandy, wrapped up and left to mature. To do this, prick the cake well with a skewer, feed periodically (weekly) with a drizzle of brandy, which will soak in through the holes. Wrap well in layers of greaseproof paper and store in an airtight container.

christmas choc-nut tartlets

These festive nut tartlets are an alternative to traditional fruit-mince pies.

pastry

1 cup flour

2 tablespoons cocoa powder

1/2 cup icing sugar

pinch salt

125g cold butter, cubed

3–4 teaspoons cold water

filling

1 cup whole macadamia nuts, lightly toasted

1 tablespoon melted butter

1/2 cup soft brown sugar

2 tablespoons golden syrup

1 small egg

100g chocolate melts to decorate

1 Place flour, cocoa, icing sugar and salt in a food processor and pulse to sift. Add cubed butter and process until crumbly. Add 3 teaspoons water and process until the mixture forms a ball of pastry (only add the fourth teaspoonful if necessary).

2 Lightly grease a 24-hole, mini-muffin pan with butter or spray with oil. Divide the pastry into 24 walnut-sized pieces and press into prepared pans to form 24 small pastry cases. Refrigerate for 30 minutes.

3 Heat oven to 180°C. Divide macadamia nuts between pastry cases. In a bowl beat melted butter, brown sugar, golden syrup and egg until smooth. Pour a little of this mixture into each nut-filled pastry case. Bake for 20–25 minutes until pastry is golden and filling is set.

4 Cool in tins for 10 minutes to firm before removing to a wire rack. Melt chocolate melts and pipe or drizzle chocolate patterns from the end of a fork to decorate tartlets.

Makes 24

+ shortcut ... make mini piping bags by twisting a triangle of greaseproof paper into a cone-shape. These are perfect for small piping jobs such as these squiggles of melted chocolate. Cleaning is easy, as they can be thrown away after use.

julie le clerc's crisp pavlova with passionfruit curd

I've always preferred a crisp-style pavlova to the more mushy versions – so that's exactly how I make mine today and it always works a treat.

4 (120ml) egg whites
1¼ cups caster sugar
1 teaspoon vanilla extract
whipped cream to decorate

1 Preheat oven to 100°C. Whisk egg whites until very stiff. Add 2 tablespoons of the sugar and continue whisking until this is incorporated.

2 Whisk in remaining sugar and vanilla for about 3 minutes, or until mixture is thick and glossy. Spoon onto an oven tray lined with non-stick baking paper and mound into desired Pavlova shape, remembering that this shape will expand a bit when it cooks. Bake for 1½ hours until crisp but not brown. Turn off the oven and leave pavlova to continue to dry out on the down-heat until the oven is cold.

3 Decorate cold pavlova as desired with whipped cream and passionfruit curd or fresh fruit such as strawberries, raspberries, mango or kiwifruit.

Serves 10

passionfruit curd

125g butter
1 cup caster sugar
juice of 2 lemons
3 eggs
4 passionfruit, pulp removed

1 Place butter, sugar and lemon juice in a heatproof bowl over a saucepan of gently simmering water. Heat until butter has melted and sugar dissolved.

2 Lightly beat eggs in another bowl. Pour first mixture over beaten eggs, whisking to incorporate.

3 Return mixture to the heatproof bowl. Stir constantly over a pan of gently simmering water until mixture will thickly coat the back of a spoon. Do not allow mixture to boil or it may curdle. Remove from the heat and stir in passionfruit pulp.

4 Ladle into hot sterilised jars and seal well. Store in a cool, dark place. Refrigerate after opening.

Makes about 2 cups

+ good idea ... under-whipped cream is more delicious to eat. Rescue slightly over-whipped cream by gently folding in a little liquid cream. If cream is whipped until it turns to butter, throw it out.

zuccotto

This dessert is a triumph! In my busy catering days, I made many a giant version of this dessert as birthday cakes. Sometimes I like to cover the whole surface in broken shards of chocolate for an even more dramatic effect.

350g trifle sponge

1/4 cup brandy

1/4 cup espresso coffee

1 cup roughly chopped quality dark chocolate

500ml (2 cups) cream

1/4 cup sifted icing sugar

2 teaspoons vanilla extract

1/3 cup chopped candied orange peel

1/3 cup chopped quality dark chocolate

cocoa powder to dust

1 Line a 1.5 litre capacity bowl with plastic wrap. Slice the trifle sponge into 5mm thick sheets. Cut the sheets into triangles. Line the bowl with the triangles of sponge, overlapping to cover the bottom and sides of bowl completely. There should be sponge left over to cover the finished zuccotto.

2 Drizzle sponge lining with brandy and espresso, reserving a little of each for the topping.

3 Melt 1 cup chocolate in a heatproof bowl over a saucepan of simmering water, or microwave in short bursts. Stir until smooth and set aside to cool. Whip cream to hold its shape. Then stir in the icing sugar, vanilla, candied orange and second measure of chopped chocolate. Spread two-thirds of this mixture over the sponge lining, leaving a space in the centre.

4 Fold the cooled melted chocolate into the remaining whipped cream mixture and use this mixture to fill the central space of the zuccotto. Cover the filling with the remaining sponge to seal it completely. Drizzle with remaining brandy and coffee.

5 Cover with plastic wrap, and place a plate on top with a weight. Refrigerate overnight. Turn out, dust with cocoa powder and serve cut in wedges.

Serves 8-10

+ good idea ... chill a bowl and whisk or beaters in the fridge before whipping cream, as the colder the cream, the faster and smoother it whips.

pashka with poached quince

Pashka is a traditional Russian Easter dessert, which is like a cream cheese studded with candied fruits, nuts and chocolate.

1 cup cream cheese at room temperature

1 cup quark

50g butter, softened

1/2 cup vanilla caster sugar (sugar stored with a vanilla pod to flavour)

1/4 cup chopped dried apricots

1/4 cup chopped quality dark chocolate

1/4 cup slivered almonds

grated rind and juice of 1 lemon

1 teaspoon vanilla extract

1 Beat cream cheese, quark, butter and sugar together until smooth. Stir in remaining ingredients.

2 Sterilise a large piece of muslin (see note below). Lay out wet muslin in a bowl and place mixture in centre. Bring together ends of cloth and tie with string. Hang from string in fridge for 24 hours to drain (over a bowl) and set.

3 Unwrap pashka and serve with poached quince or fresh fruit.

Serves 10

poached quince

2 litres water

4 cups sugar

1 cinnamon stick

peeled zest and juice of 1 lemon

5 quinces, peeled, quartered and cored

1 Place water, sugar, cinnamon stick, lemon zest and juice in a large saucepan and bring to the boil, stirring until sugar dissolves.

2 Add quince, turn down the heat to a gentle simmer and cook for 3–4 hours without stirring. The longer the fruit cooks, the darker colour it will become. Remove quince and syrup to a bowl to cool.

3 Remove the quince from the syrup and boil the syrup to reduce it to a thick glaze if desired. Serve with pashka.

Serves 10

+ how to ... sterilise muslin. It's not as complicated as it sounds! Place muslin cloth in a saucepan of boiling water and boil for 5 minutes. Remove, cool and wring out muslin, which is now sterilised and ready for use.

florentine slice

Lining the tin with non-stick baking paper to come up the sides has a dual purpose – this prevents the slice from sticking to the tin, and provides nifty handles to pull for easy removal.

100g butter

½ cup tightly packed brown sugar

⅓ cup golden syrup

⅔ cup plain flour

1 cup raisins

1 cup chopped candied fruit, such as apricots, pineapple, papaya

100g sliced (flaked) almonds

½ cup toasted hazelnuts

200g dark chocolate melts, to ice

1 Preheat oven to 180°C on fan bake. Line a 27 x 17cm slice tin with non-stick baking paper.

2 Combine butter, brown sugar and golden syrup in a saucepan and bring to the boil, stirring until sugar dissolves. Remove from the heat and stir in flour, then fruit and nuts. Pour mixture into prepared tin and spread evenly. Bake for 25 minutes or until golden brown.

3 Cool for a while in the tin before turning out to cool completely.

4 Melt chocolate in a bowl over a pan of simmering water, or microwave in short bursts. Stir until smooth, then spread on underside of cold slice. Leave to set, then cut into bars.

Makes 16

+ good idea ... cut slices in different ways for good effect – bars and squares work well for lunch-box treats; diamonds or triangles are sophisticated; and tiny bite-sized cubes make great after-dinner nibbles with coffee.

+ my advice ... if white streaks or powdery blotches appear on chocolate this is known as 'bloom'. Humidity can produce a sugar bloom and excessive heat a sweaty fat bloom. Bloom doesn't affect flavour but is best avoided by storing chocolate in a cool, dry place.

pecan, prune and chocolate celebration cake

I've forgotten exactly how the sentiment goes, but someone once said that one of the most thoughtful gifts is the gift of time. Take the time to bake this incredibly special celebration cake for someone you love.

½ cup roughly chopped pitted prunes

½ cup brandy

250g roughly chopped quality dark chocolate

150g butter

3 eggs, separated

¾ cup caster sugar

½ cup plain flour

¾ cup finely ground pecan nuts (or substitute
  ground almonds)

1 Place prunes and brandy in a bowl, cover and leave to soak overnight.

2 Next day, preheat oven to 160°C on fan bake. Grease and flour a 22cm springform cake tin and line the base with non-stick baking paper. Place chocolate and butter in a bowl and melt over a saucepan of gently simmering water, or microwave in short bursts.

3 Place egg yolks and sugar in a bowl and beat with an electric mixer until thick and pale. Stir in melted chocolate and butter. Gently stir in flour, ground nuts, prunes and soaking liquid.

4 Whisk egg whites until they form soft peaks, then carefully fold into cake mixture. Pour into prepared cake tin and bake for 45–60 minutes or until cake tests cooked when a skewer inserted comes out moist but clean.

5 Cool cake for a while in tin before turning out on a wire rack. Ice with chocolate ganache (see page 104).

Serves 10

index

aioli, corn and dill **63**
amazing christmas cake **152**
angel hair pasta with smoked tuna and lemon **133**
antipasto salad **70**
aperol and raspberry jelly **111**
artichoke and bacon strata **122**
asparagus spears with purple olive cream **43**
avocado and bacon burgers **33**

baby pappadams holding curried scallops **40**
baby potatoes with sour cream and salmon caviar **46**
bacon and avocado burgers **33**
bacon, and artichoke strata **122**
baked penne, beef and mushroom layers **124**
beef, baked penne and mushroom layers **124**
beef, rare on rye with horseradish cream **43**
beef, roast, with merlot mushroom sauce **94**
beetroot, warm chorizo and feta salad **134**
bread cups filled with salmon and kaffir lime salad **38**
broccoli and parmesan risotto **26**
burnt sugar tarts **117**

cake, amazing christmas **152**
cake, chocolate swirl sliver **100**
cake, greek yoghurt, honey and orange syrup **107**
cake, pecan, prune and chocolate celebration **162**
cake, vanilla pear and pistachio **109**
cakes, espresso and chocolate croissant pudding **104**
caramelised lemon julienne **116**
caramel sauce **102**
carrot dip, spiced **37**
cheesecakes, free-form cherry **112**
cherry, free-form cheesecakes **112**
chicken and spinach salad with japanese-style dressing **72**
chicken and vegetables with fragrant peanut sauce **128**
chicken jambalaya **27**
chicken with chorizo, tomato and bay leaves **84**
chicken, coconut salad in a leaf **72**
chicken, curried thai pies **30**
chicken, grilled, with north african eggplant salad **30**
chicken, macadamia and lentil salad **127**
chicken, oven-dried tomato and couscous **28**
chicken, petit coq au vin **88**
chicken, roast with chestnut and apple stuffing **144**
chicken, slow-cooked ginger **84**
chicken schnitzel with cherry tomato and rocket sauce **128**
chicken, thai curried pies **30**
choc-nut, christmas tartlets **155**
chocolate, hot, with cinnamon **138**
chocolate ganache **104**
chocolate swirl sliver cake **100**
chocolate, espresso croissant pudding cakes **104**
chocolate pudding, hazelnut self-saucing **99**

chocolate, pecan prune celebration cake **162**
chocolate pots, dark **99**
chorizo, warm, beetroot and feta salad **134**
chorizo, with chicken, tomato and bay leaves **84**
chowder, classic seafood **136**
christmas cake, amazing **152**
christmas choc-nut tartlets **155**
cinnamon hot chocolate **138**
classic seafood chowder **136**
coconut chicken salad in a leaf **72**
courgette and parmesan soup **75**
coq au vin, petit **88**
creole gumbo **122**
crisp duck with dried cranberry sauce **144**
crostini **37**
crushed pea pasta with chargrilled lamb cutlets **18**
curried-chicken pies, thai **30**
curry, fragrant vegetable **89**
curry, red lamb **17**

dark chocolate pots **99**
dip, feta and fennel seed **37**
dip, spiced carrot **37**
dressing, asian-inspired **149**
dressing, coconut **72**
dressing, lemon coriander **30**
dressing, lime **64**
dressing, japanese-style **72**
dressing, toasted pine nut **147**
duck, crisp with dried cranberry sauce **144**
duck, szechuan-spiced twice-roasted **82**

eggplant, pepper, courgette and feta terrine **70**
espresso and chocolate croissant pudding cakes **104**

feta and fennel seed dip **37**
feta, warm chorizo and beetroot salad **134**
fig and ginger puddings **102**
figs with gorgonzola and prosciutto **38**
fish baked with oregano and tomato juice **24**
fish balls, spicy, on baby lettuce leaves **44**
fish pie, smoked, with parsley mash **24**
fish salad, lime-marinated **69**
florentine slice **161**
fragrant lemon rice **84**
fragrant peanut sauce **128**
fragrant vegetable curry **89**
free-form cherry cheesecakes **112**
frittata, pumpkin and salami **27**

garlic, peeling **128**
gazpacho salsa, with oysters **54**
gazpacho, shots of clear **50**

glaze, mustard and apricot **142**
glazed ham on the bone **142**
goats' cheese and oven-dried tomatoes in basil leaves **50**
goats' cheese, warm prosciutto-wrapped and
  roast pear salad **66**
goulash, mushroom **124**
greek meatballs with tomato and olive sauce **21**
greek yoghurt, honey and orange syrup cake **107**
gremalada **90**
gumbo, creole **122**

ham, glazed **142**
ham, how to store **142**
hazelnut pesto **66**
hokkien noodles with tofu and water chestnuts **33**
horseradish cream with rare beef on rye **43**
hot toddy **138**

jelly, aperol and raspberry **111**
julie le clerc's crisp pavlova with passionfruit curd **156**

kir **54**

lamb, carrot and ginger dumplings, steamed **46**
lamb cutlets, chargrilled, with crushed pea pasta **18**
lamb shanks with field mushrooms **14**
lamb, leg, marinated butterflied with pineapple salsa **148**
lamb, red curry **17**
lamb rack, sun-dried tomato and olive-coated **92**
lemon julienne, caramelised **116**
lemon rice **84**
lentil, and macadamia chicken salad **127**
lentils, pinot noir, with saffron tuna **80**
lentils, puy, how to cook **94**
lime-marinated fish salad **69**
limoncello mousse **116**

macadamia chicken and lentil salad **127**
macadamia steamed puddings with caramel sauce **102**
margarita **57**
marinated butterflied leg of lamb with pineapple salsa **148**
mashed potatoes, great **80**
mayonnaise, wasabi and lime with tuna kebabs **42**
meatballs, greek with tomatoes and olives **21**
milanese-style risotto **90**
mousse, limoncello **116**
mushroom goulash **124**
mussels poached in sparkling wine **64**
mustard-crusted salmon with asparagus and lemon sauce **82**

north african eggplant salad with grilled chicken **30**

olive cream, purple **43**

olive paste quesadillas **40**
orange syrup **107**
osso buco al pomodoro with milanese-style risotto **90**
oven-dried tomato and chicken couscous **28**
oven-dried tomatoes **28**
oven-dried tomatoes and goats' cheese in basil leaves **50**
oysters with gazpacho salsa **54**

pannacotta, vanilla with pineapple and
  passionfruit salad **119**
paprika pork with potatoes and spinach **136**
parmesan shortbread, how to make **53**
pashka with poached quince **158**
passionfruit curd **156**
pasta, angel hair with smoked tuna and lemon **133**
pasta, crushed pea with chargrilled lamb cutlets **18**
pavlova, crisp with passionfruit curd **156**
peanut sauce, fragrant **128**
pecan, prune and chocolate celebration cake **162**
pesto potatoes **144**
pesto, hazelnut **66**
petit coq au vin **88**
pickled fennel and cucumber **130**
pineapple and passionfruit salad **119**
plum sago pudding **116**
pork and raisin rolls with salsa verde **49**
pork fillet wrapped in pears and bacon **94**
pork, paprika with potatoes and spinach **136**
potatoes, baby, with sour cream and salmon caviar **46**
prawn rice paper rolls **62**
prawn salad, with shaved corn and rocket and dill aioli **63**
prawns with coconut and coriander dipping sauce **60**
prosciutto-wrapped goats' cheese and
  roast pear warm salad **66**
pudding, plum sago **116**
pudding, self-saucing chocolate hazelnut **99**
puddings, fig and ginger **102**
puddings, steamed macadamia with caramel sauce **102**
pumpkin and salami frittata **27**
purple olive cream **43**
puy lentils, how to cook **94**

quesadillas, olive paste **40**
quince, poached with pashka **158**

rare beef on rye with horseradish cream **43**
raspberry jelly, and aperol **111**
red lamb curry **17**
red pepper purée **18**
risotto, broccoli and parmesan **26**
risotto, milanese-style with osso buco al pomodoro **90**
rissoles, salmon with pickled fennel and cucumber **130**
roast beef with merlot mushroom sauce **94**

roast chicken with chestnut and apple stuffing **144**
roast peppers, how to **70**
roast salmon **149**
roast turkey and dried peach salad with
  toasted pine nut dressing **147**
rose turkish delight trifle **111**

saffron tuna with pinot noir lentils **80**
sago pudding, plum **116**
salad, bread cups filled with salmon and kaffir lime **38**
salad caprise **75**
salad, antipasto **70**
salad, chicken and spinach **72**
salad, coconut chicken in a leaf **72**
salad, macadamia chicken and lentil **127**
salad, lime-marinated fish **69**
salad, north african eggplant with grilled chicken **30**
salad, pasta with tuna, feta and rocket **133**
salad, pineapple and passionfruit with
  vanilla pannacotta **119**
salad, roast turkey and dried peach with
  toasted pine nut dressing **147**
salad, scallop and courgette **64**
salad, shaved corn, prawn and rocket with
  corn and dill aioli **63**
salad, warm chorizo, beetroot and feta **134**
salad, warm prosciutto-wrapped goats' cheese and
  roast pear **66**
salmon rissoles with pickled fennel and cucumber **130**
salmon with asian-inspired dressing and
  green vegetable medley **149**
salmon, bread cups **38**
salmon, mustard-crusted with asparagus and
  lemon sauce **82**
salmon, teriyaki **69**
salsa verde, with pork and raisin rolls **49**
salsa, gazpacho **54**
salsa, pineapple **148**
sangria, strawberry **57**
sauce, caramel **102**
sauce, cherry tomato and rocket **128**
sauce, coconut and coriander dipping **60**
sauce, dried cranberry **144**
sauce, fragrant peanut **128**
sauce, lemon **82**
sauce, merlot mushroom **94**
sauce, tomato and olive **21**
sauce, sage and caper with veal **142**
scallop and courgette salad **64**
scallops in the half-shell with hazelnut pesto **66**
scallops, curried in baby pappadams **40**
seafood stew with couscous **22**
seafood chowder, classic **136**

self-saucing chocolate hazelnut pudding **99**
shaved corn, prawn and rocket salad with corn and
  dill aioli **63**
shots of clear gazpacho **50**
slice, florentine **161**
slow-cooked ginger chicken **84**
smoked fish pie with parsley mash **24**
snapper with sweet and sour onions **80**
soup, courgette and parmesan **75**
spiced carrot dip **37**
spicy fish balls on baby lettuce leaves **44**
spinach, and chicken salad with
  japanese-style dressing **72**
steamed lamb, carrot and ginger dumplings **46**
stew, seafood with couscous **22**
strata, artichoke and bacon **122**
strawberry sangria **57**
stuffing, chestnut and apple **144**
sun-dried tomato and olive-coated rack of lamb **92**
sweet potato gratin **14**
szechuan-spiced twice-roasted duck **82**

tartlets, christmas choc-nut **155**
tarts, burnt sugar **117**
teriyaki salmon **69**
terrine, eggplant, pepper, courgette and feta **70**
thai curried-chicken pies **30**
toddy, hot **138**
tofu, and water chestnuts with hokkien noodles **33**
trifle, rose turkish delight **111**
tuna kebabs with wasabi and lime mayonnaise **42**
tuna, feta, rocket and pasta salad **133**
tuna, saffron with pinot noir lentils **80**
tuna, smoked with angel hair pasta and lemon **133**
turkey, roast, with dried peach salad with
  toasted pine nut dressing **147**
turkish delight trifle, rose **111**

vanilla beans **119**
vanilla custard **117**
vanilla pannacotta with pineapple and passionfruit salad **119**
vanilla pear and pistachio cake **109**
vanilla pears **109**
veal with sage and caper sauce **142**
vegetable curry, fragrant **89**
vegetable, green medley **149**
vegetable stock **89**

warm chorizo, beetroot and feta salad **134**
warm prosciutto-wrapped goats' cheese and
  roast pear salad **66**

zuccotto **157**

PENGUIN BOOKS
Published by the Penguin Group
Penguin Group (NZ), cnr Airborne and Rosedale Roads,
Albany, Auckland 1310, New Zealand
Penguin Books Ltd, 80 Strand,
London, WC2R 0RL, England
Penguin Group (USA) Inc., 375 Hudson Street,
New York, NY 10014, United States
Penguin Group (Australia), 250 Camberwell Road,
Camberwell, Victoria 3124, Australia
Penguin Books Canada Ltd, 10 Alcorn Avenue,
Toronto, Ontario, Canada M4V 3B2
Penguin Books (South Africa) (Pty) Ltd, 24 Sturdee Avenue,
Rosebank, Johannesburg 2196, South Africa
Penguin Books India (P) Ltd, 11, Community Centre,
Panchsheel Park, New Delhi 110 017, India
Penguin Ireland Ltd, 25 St Stephen's Green,
Dublin 2, Ireland

Penguin Books Ltd, Registered Offices:
80 Strand, London, WC2R 0RL, England

First published by Penguin Group (NZ), 2004
1 3 5 7 9 10 8 6 4 2

Copyright © text, Julie Le Clerc, 2004
Copyright © photographs, Penguin Books (NZ) and Julie Le Clerc

The right of Julie Le Clerc to be identified as the author of
this work in terms of section 96 of the Copyright Act 1994
is hereby asserted.

Food photography by Bruce Nicholson
Incidental photography by Julie Le Clerc
Designed and typeset by Athena Sommerfeld
Prepress by microdot
Printed in China through Bookbuilders

All rights reserved. Without limiting the rights under copyright
reserved above, no part of this publication may be reproduced,
stored in or introduced into a retrieval system, or transmitted, in
any form or by any means (electronic, mechanical, photocopying,
recording or otherwise), without the prior written permission of
both the copyright owner and the above publisher of this book.

ISBN 0 14 301928 7
A catalogue record for this book is available
from the National Library of New Zealand.

www.penguin.co.nz
www.julieleclerc.com